THE STORY OF TERRY'S

THE STORY OF TERRY'S

Van Wilson

YORK ORAL HISTORY SOCIETY 2009

© Van Wilson 2009

Published By York Oral History Society 2009

ISBN 978-0-9513652-5-0

Cover design and photograph on front cover by Toby Wilson

Photos on back cover – Terry's All Gold Balloon 1975
                        Hill's factory operate at Terry's 1944
                        Terry's Van

Prepared by:

York Publishing Services Ltd
64 Hallfield Road
Layerthorpe
York YO31 7ZQ
Tel: 01904 431213

Website: www.yps-publishing.co.uk

CONTENTS

INTRODUCTION

A long chapter of York's history ended when Terry's chocolate factory closed in 2005. It had gone through many changes since the 1960s, when the company was first taken over by Forte's, some good changes, some not so good. When the company closed, its archive was split. The Borthwick Institute received most of the photographs, plus documents and memorabilia. The York Castle Museum received a lot of the packaging and other items, and Kraft Foods took away part of the archive to their head office. At this point, the Castle Museum contacted us and suggested we carry out an oral history project and talk to people who had worked or had some involvement with Terry's. A newspaper article brought in a very good response and we contacted other people who we knew were still around. Unfortunately we were unable to talk to Peter Terry as he was very ill at that stage, and died a few months later. Subsequently I have been able to interview Anthony Terry, Peter's eldest son and the only one of his family to work at Terry's, and I was also given access to Darrell Buttery's recorded interview with Peter Terry from 2004, and John Shannon's interview with Noel Terry from the late 1970s.

Over the next few months, we talked to a wide range of Terry's people, ranging from directors to factory and office workers, bakers and chefs, engineers, joiners and electricians, marketing staff and reps. Everyone we spoke to described Terry's as a family firm, one which cared for its employees. Despite takeovers, and the politics which exist in all companies, the general picture painted was one of a happy place. Even in the turbulent period of the 1970s, when industry was affected by strikes and disruptions, the workforce at Terry's retained a strong loyalty to both the firm and the family.

But of course as Terry's neared its final days, feelings were raw and there is still, even today, a real sense of sadness and loss at the closure of a company which had been a major employer in York for over 200 years. Terry's did not only sell confectionery, but they also sold romance, luxury, real pleasure.

To quote from the 1967 Terry's Bicentenary book produced for employees,

'There is a universal appeal, and a sort of innocence, about confectionery. Children handing over hot, clutched pocket money, young men treating their girlfriends to that first half pound assortment, husbands hastily remembering their wives and sons their mothers, so much harmless pleasure seems to reflect back upon the makers. It is an industry over which there permanently hangs the sweet smell of chocolate, and round any corner of which one may suddenly come across a vast copper full of cherries, a flagon of Cointreau, or a tub of honey'.

This publication does not purport to be a comprehensive record of confectionery making. This has been covered elsewhere. It is not a technical manual, although there is reference to the manufacture of chocolate and the different processes involved. Instead this is a record of memories of those who worked in the many different areas of Terry's, accompanied by extensive background research and a wonderful collection of photographs. It is dedicated to all those who have worked at Terry's, and to the Terry family past and present.

ACKNOWLEDGEMENTS

A publication such as this is never the work of one single person. I am very grateful to the York Castle Museum, in particular Sherri Steel, curator of social history, for originally commissioning us to carry out the oral history interviews, and for their support with the project. We are greatly indebted to the following for their financial grants to enable us to produce the book and exhibition –

Grantside Developments (in particular Steve Davis, the Managing Director), the Sheldon Memorial Trust, the Noel Terry Charitable Trust and Brian and Mary Wilson.

I wish to thank Darrell Buttery for his interview with Peter Terry, and Rita Freedman, the archivist, and the Merchant Adventurers' Company, for the recording of Noel Terry. The Borthwick Institute, York City Archives and the York Reference Library were all very helpful with research. Thanks to David Poole who helped with individual questions, and Steve Hanson of Image Computers/Graphic Design who made a good job of scanning our photographs. Thanks also to Henry Robertson for conducting an interview, and to Kraft for their support.

Particular thanks go to Mike Grimes for lending and copying photographs and brochures, as well as answering queries. Many thanks to Toby Wilson for his design of the book's cover and to York Publishing Services.

My thanks go to the committee of York Oral History Society, in particular our treasurer Alan Hardwick.

Special thanks to Mike Race for his huge contribution, interviewing and transcribing, helping with research, copying photographs, liaising and working with the printers, and proofreading the manuscript. His help has been invaluable and essential to this project.

Most of all, our thanks go to the many people who shared their stories and experiences of Terry's with us –

Jacqueline Ake (daughter of Ernest Clayton), Nick Banks, Sandra Barnes, Alan Benson, Peter Binns, Vic Botterill, Charles Braithwaite, George Bradley, Pauline Bradley, Agnes Bridgewood, Jenny Briggs, Sylvia Brough, Eileen Carter, Cissie Colley, Dorothy Cowan, Tony Coward Lawrence (Lol) Cussons, Max Drucquer, John Earnshaw, Terry and Moira Ellis, Sheila Elmer, Nancy Fairbotham, Bill Godfrey, Maurice Grimes, Mike Grimes, Elsie Hall, Betty Hartas, Richard Harte, Anne Horner, Eve Hudson, Ian Johnston, Audrey & Tony Lambert, Alice Leaf, Jean Lindsay, Irene McGouran, David Meek, Betty Metcalfe, Winnie Mothersdale, Mabel Nicholson, Joan Pannett, Elsie Reed and her daughter Lynne Townend, Anne Ruttle, Ethel Smith, Joe Smith, Janet Starkey, Kath Stokoe, Anthony Terry, Fred Thomas, Doreen Varrie, Brian and Jean Winship.-

BOOKS BY THE SAME AUTHOR

The History of a Community : Fulford Road District of York.
University College of Ripon and York St John. 1984. Reprinted 1985.

Alexina : A Woman in Wartime York. 1995

Rich in all but Money : Life in Hungate 1900-1938. *York Archaeological Trust.*
1996. Reprinted 1997. New edition 2007

Beyond the Postern Gate : A History of Fishergate and Fulford Road. *York Archaeological Trust.* 1996

Humour, Heartache and Hope : Life in Walmgate. *York Archaeological Trust.*
1996

York Memories. *Tempus Publishing.* 1998

Number 26 : The History of 26 St Saviourgate. *Voyager Publications.* 1999

Voices of St Paul's : An Oral History of St Paul's, Holgate. (Edited).
William Sessions 2001

Rhythm and Romance : An Oral History of Popular Music in York. Volume 1 :
The Dance Band Years. *York Oral History Society.* 2002

Something in the Air : An Oral History of Popular Music in York. Volume 2 :
The Beat Goes On. *York Oral History Society* 2002

The Walmgate Story. *Voyager Publications* 2006. Reprinted 2009

Rations, Raids and Romance : York in the Second World War.
York Archaeological Trust. 2008

Stonegate Voices. *York Archaeological Trust.* 2009

CHAPTER ONE

IN THE BEGINNING

1767. King George III was on the British throne, and while the legal campaign against slavery was beginning, and British explorer Samuel Wallis was discovering Tahiti, two York men, William Bayldon and Robert Berry, decided to open a shop close to Bootham Bar selling cough lozenges, citron, lemon and orange candied peel and other sweetmeats. The 18th century was a productive time, and one of great social and cultural changes. Globally, American was soon to gain its independence, and the Russian and Danish had formed a treaty, though Russia was soon to be at war with Turkey. Fortunately there had been an Anglo-Russian treaty of friendship, commerce and navigation the previous year. The world was expanding, with James Cook planning his first voyage to the Antipodes in the Endeavour. These global links would prove useful in the years to come.

Nearer to home, there were advances in industry, with James Hargreaves and the 'Spinning Jenny', and James Watt inventing a condenser for the steam engine. Culturally, 1767 saw the earliest record of a piano in England, Rousseau wrote his Dictionary of Music, and the first volumes of the Encyclopaedia Britannica were produced. Samuel Johnson had founded his Literary Club in 1764, and Joshua Reynolds became the first president of the Royal Academy of Arts in 1768. In York, the Mansion House, Assembly Rooms, and the County Hospital had all been built in the second and third decades of the century. Coffee houses and booksellers abounded, and the two York newspapers, the York Mercury and the York Courant, had been founded in 1719 and 1725 respectively.

In 1823, Joseph Terry, a 30 year old man whose father was a farmer in Pocklington, joined Bayldon and Berry's business. He had been trained as an apothecary and it is said that through this training he learnt to 'sugar the pill'. This stood him in good stead because he brought to the business high principles and a desire for quality in the products. In 1813 he was advertising in the York Courant, his new business 'opposite the Castle, selling spices, pickling vinegar, essence of spruce, patent medicines and perfumery'. He then moved to Walmgate and dealt in herbs, spices, drugs and lozenges, as well as conducting phlebotomy and keeping a jar of leeches in his window. In the same year, he married Harriet Atkinson who was the niece of Robert Berry. Robert's son George also joined the business. So there was now a family connection. Bayldon and Berry described Terry as a 'benign man' with 'a kindly attitude to others...courteous, fair and seeking the best'.

In 1824, the firm, now Joseph Terry's, moved from Bootham into St Helen's Square. (This building later became the Terry's restaurant, and now belongs to the Lloyds TSB bank. Several shops have leased it and it is now the Swarovski jewellers). Robert Berry had died and Bayldon had left the business. The Yorkshire Gazette of 29th October 1825 read,

Joseph Terry and George Berry, confectioners, St Helen's Square, having taken the Stock and entered upon the premises of the late Robert Berry and Co, most respectfully solicit both from the Friends of the late Firm and from the Public at large, that Patronage so liberally bestowed on their Predecessors, which they will ever faithfully and anxiously endeavour to merit. All Persons to whom the late Mr Robert Berry stood indebted, at the time of his decease, are requested to forward their accounts, with the securities for the same, without delay, in order that they may be discharged : and all Persons indebted to the late Firm, are desired immediately to pay the amount of their accounts to Messrs Terry and Berry.

J Terry respectfully acknowledges the very liberal Patronage bestowed upon him for the last Ten Years as Chemist and Druggist, in his late Situation in Walmgate, and informs his Friends and the Public that, having entered on the Business lately carried on by the late Robert Berry and Co, Confectioners, St Helen's Square, he has disposed of the Stock of Drugs &c to Mr R Tonge, for whom he begs to solicit future favours.

Joseph Terry, founder of Terry's
(Courtesy Mike Grimes)

Two years later, Terry decided to expand the firm's products to include more confectionery. The partnership between Berry and Terry dissolved and Joseph found himself alone, working from St Helen's

Square, with the factory in Brearly Yard. As well as boiled sweets of different kinds, he also produced comfits, medicated lozenges, marmalade, mushroom ketchup and the original of the modern 'love hearts' which bore a likeness of Prince Albert and the Crystal Palace and had messages such as, 'Can you polka?' and 'How do you flirt?' on them.

Unfortunately, after leaving the business, George Berry's health went downhill. The Yorkshire Gazette of 23rd December 1848, reported on an inquest held at the Flying Horse in Coppergate. George had lived in nearby Mason's Buildings and on this particular Sunday he had not attended the parish church to receive an allowance of bread, as he usually did, so a neighbour investigated and found him dead. His death was caused by heart disease and the verdict returned was that he 'died by visitation from God'.

The advent of the railway in the early nineteenth century made it much easier for goods to be taken further afield. The Terry's representative's leather bound sales ledger of 1826 covered Barnsley, Barton, Bawtry, Beverley, Brigg, Caistor, Doncaster, Gainsborough, Hatfield, Horncastle, Hull, Lincoln, Retford, Rotherham, Selby, Sheffield, Snaith, South Milford, Thorne, Tickhill, Wath, Winteringham, Winterton, Worksop and Wragby. By 1840 Terry's products were being sent to 75 towns all over the north of England, the Midlands, and as far south as London. They included 'candied citron, mint cakes, candied eringo, coltsfoot rock, anchovies, gum balls, pomfret cakes, and lozenges made from squill, camphor and horehound'. The 1836 prospectus of the Association for the Protection of Public and Trade of Confectioners and Lozenge Makers, reports on the general meeting at the George and Vulture Tavern, Lombard Street held in March and mentions that Mr Joseph Terry was on the committee. There must have been some fraudulent businesses around as the association was formed 'to protect against individuals manufacturing or vending lozenges and confectionery composed of injurious materials'. Subscriptions were one guinea p.a. or a donation of £5.5s. Joseph Terry gave the latter.

Having transformed the confectioner's from its humble beginnings, Joseph Terry died in 1850. There were many bequests in his will, including some generous annuities for servants. He had five sons (and three daughters) and three of them went into the business, Joseph, Robert and John. But it was Joseph junior who was to take the company forward, even though he was only 22 when his father died. In 1862 the works were moved to a new site at Clementhorpe, close to the river where there was space for warehouses to store all the stock. The workers were

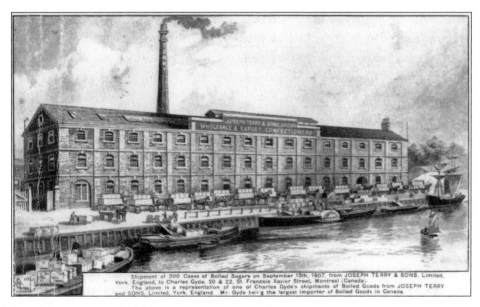

Clementhorpe September 1907. Shipment of 200 cases of boiled sugars from Terry's to Montreal, Canada.

(Courtesy Mike Grimes)

transferred from St Helen's Square to Clementhorpe between Autumn 1863 and Spring 1864 but it was not until 1886 that the firm had a factory specifically for making chocolate.

Chocolate had actually arrived in England in 1650 and Samuel Pepys recorded in his diary that 'jocolatte is very good'. At this time it was a drink, and something which only the rich could afford. As well as the popular coffee houses in the 18th century, chocolate houses also sprang up but eating chocolate did not appear until the late 1840s. It came originally from the ancient Aztec and Maya civilisations of South and Central America who drank 'chocolatl' made from cocoa beans, and it was the Spanish explorers, or conquistadors, who discovered and took away with them, the Theobroma Cacoa, the 'food of the gods'. Before long, it had spread throughout Europe and further afield.

By 1867, Terry's were selling over 400 items, including 13 different kinds of chocolate creams, batons, medallions and tablets. So a firm which had begun with boiled sweets, eventually became predominantly manufacturers of chocolate, unlike the other major chocolate manufacturers in the UK, Cadbury's, Fry's (which later merged with Cadbury's) and Rowntree's, who all began with chocolate production. Terry's catalogue for 1874 offered lozenges (bismuth, blackcurrant, cinnamon, clove, lemon, lavender, vanilla and violet), candies (acidulated drops, toffee tablets, Indian sugar sticks, orange slices), preserved fruits (apricots in syrup, dried cherries) and pate de jujubes (pine, rose, strawberry), as well as various liqueurs, comfits, peels, cakes, biscuits and jams, with chocolate cigars, cream balls and chocolate cream cakes at a halfpenny and a penny. It was said that the firm catered for the rich county families who always had their tables laden with a wealth of variety in confectionery.

Joseph Terry II became well known in York, and, as well as being Sheriff, actually served as Lord Mayor four times, (1874, 1885, 1886, and 1890), one of only a few men to do so. In 1893, he resigned from the city council but after widespread protests, agreed to return. Terry's knighthood for services to industry was conferred in 1887 after he represented the city at Queen Victoria's Golden Jubilee. He was also Chairman of the Yorkshire Gala Committee, the Council's representative on the board of governors of Yorkshire Fine Art and Industrial Institution, a member of the board of Bootham Asylum, governor of the Merchant Adventurers' Company, member of York Race Committee, vice president of York Musical Society, deputy chairman of York New Waterworks Company, and supporter of York Charity Organisation Society. In 1893, he

Sir Joseph Terry when Lord Mayor for third time in 1886.
(Courtesy Borthwick Institute)

presided over a Japanese bazaar, in aid of the York Central Mission, which took place in the Exhibition Building, behind the Art Gallery. Terry said, 'It is right to think of our poorer neighbours. If the bazaar is successful, then 1000 waifs and strays would be entertained on Christmas Day in the Corn Exchange'. In 1895 the firm became a limited company. It was the age of the Industrial Exhibition and Terry's received medals at a number of exhibitions between 1866 and 1900, bronze, silver and gold. The latter was won at the National Temperance Catering Exhibition of 1899.

In 1895, shares in the company were split between Sir Joseph Terry, his wife Margaret, his elder son Thomas, Thomas's wife Sarah, the younger son Samuel Saville Terry, Frances Harriet Terry, the accountant Henry Gaskell Blackburn and solicitor William Walker.

Although the second youngest of the Terry brothers, Sir Joseph outlived them all and when he died in 1898, the Yorkshire Herald reported, 'There was no person in the city more loved and respected, and no-one who was more possessed of the qualities that constitute a genial and amiable Englishman'. But there were others who were ready to pick up the baton. Joseph had married twice. Firstly in 1854 to Frances Goddard who died in 1866, having produced three sons, and secondly to Margaret Thorpe in 1871, producing one son and three daughters. Joseph's eldest son Thomas Walker Leaper Terry had become a governing director, and then Francis Terry, known as Frank, Joseph's son by his second marriage, joined the firm in 1903 aged twenty five and was later the Chairman for 35 years, becoming Sir Francis Terry. It was Thomas who was instrumental in taking the Terry name to Australia and New Zealand, where the exports were packed in large square metal cases which were then used as water tanks by Australian farmers, and he was a founder member of the Manufacturing Confectioners' Alliance. He was a keen cyclist and was killed in 1910 after a collision with a horse and trap. The Clementhorpe works grew from strength to strength. One of the reasons for the success of the business was its close proximity to the river, which provided an excellent transport system for the city. By 1890 the firm had 300 employees who worked 59 hours beginning the working day at 6am. These long hours and difficult conditions made 153 of them sign their names in 1894 to a 'Round Robin' petitioning for

> the shortning of the hours of labour, namely nine hours movement. We are seeking that rest and recreation which is enjoyed by all other trades and professions.

George Battrick became an office boy at Terry's in October 1895, eventually serving the company for 50 years. He recalls,

> There were 20 lady clerks or typists, working nine to six. From January to March when the stock books had to be priced and ledgers balanced, there was overtime unpaid for four or five nights a week as a general rule. Sugar, almonds, peel and gum came by steamers from Hull and Goole, and coal by barge from the Castleford area. There were many cargoes of sugar, as products were made from pure cane sugar only. They never used glucose in boiling. There were three travellers from Terry's, one for Birmingham down to Portsmouth, one for Manchester and Liverpool, and

Early 1900s staff
(Courtesy Borthwick Institute)

Packing shop c1900
(Courtesy Borthwick Institute)

one for Newcastle to Yorkshire. We had a substantial export trade to Australia, New Zealand, South Africa and later Canada. Raw goods, lozenges and cachous were sent in 600 gallon galvanised iron tanks. We imported peel from Italy, which came by sea to Hull, packed in brine in hogs' heads. One ship was wrecked off the Humber, and the insurance company offered £1 for each hog's head washed ashore. Mr Tom [Thomas Terry] went to Italy to see it packed and shipped.

My first job was to index the letter book. All letters were copied by using damp cloths and a hand press. Letters were written in copying ink with a very thick nib. We had to answer Sir Joseph's bell. The oldest female employee, Mary Davis, came down from the girls' packing room each morning to see if he wanted the usual glass of milk and a bun. Then the police court sergeant would come to say if he was wanted for the magistrate's court. There was a phone on the premises in the general office, a strong room with ledgers and drug and essence stores. Every morning trays of 'cots' (small white pots representing our boiling) were brought in from the boiling room and other departments for Mr Tom [to taste]. Once a fortnight the factory doctor came in and looked at any new employees. Space had to be cleared for him. In 1895, there were 200 employees, mostly women and girls. Many wore shawls, well worn cotton stockings and boots. It was piece work, usually 12/6d or 17/6d a week. Workmen started at eighteen shillings. In 1896 and '97, the directors took all the employees to Scarborough then Bridlington.

George Battrick 1922
(Courtesy Borthwick Institute)

After a few months, I did invoicing, then posting ledgers, then a short spell in the stores and drug distribution, purchases and wages. Then I was in charge of St Helen's books in 1898, just after the sudden death of Sir Joseph. I spent the morning of the funeral at Hawthorn Villa, taking in the many wreaths and recording names.

In 1899 we ran a children's paint book competition. Pictures to be painted were outlines of some of our showcards. We had 20,000 applications! There was a rush on printing them and our small office staff had to cope!

Miss Holgate managed St Helen's after the death of its manager in 1899. The shop had a few tea tables.

All the cakes were brought daily from the bakehouse by Joe Kendall in his one horse van. They decided to re-model and extend St Helen's to be a fully equipped first class restaurant. It was managed by Mr Ware from London. The first chef was Charles Aldridge and the first head waiter was Mr Ingham. I was put in charge of the front shop and spent three years in a frock coat, with six girls behind the counter and two waitresses. Morning coffee was starting to be fashionable. We would ground our own beans, two thirds Costa Rica and one third Peaberry, with real cream. The chocolate reputation started from St Helen's. There was a heavy postal demand from all over the UK. Chocolate nougat was in boxes, the lids padded in cotton wool. We bought Christmas boxes from Hoffman and Tiede of Berlin. Mr Hoffman came round every February with samples and the boxes came in July. They ranged from 7/6d to 40s, tied with huge bows of ribbons. The packing started in October.

When Frank Terry came, there were lots of developments and new lines including caramels, vanilla hearts and rum truffles. It was my suggestion to have chocolate mint creams. Durham University rugger team, after a match with St Peter's School, swarmed into the shop on the way to the station and bought 32 pounds of crystallised mint creams.

Restaurant staff pre 1900
(Courtesy Borthwick Institute)

Our takings varied. The lowest cash taking was a snowy February day, when we took £6, and the best was the Saturday before Christmas, £200. In 1902-3, the shop and restaurant made a profit of £2000. A lady customer for many years ordered a cake to weigh as much as her age, in one cake with no tiers. When she got over 60, it had to be baked in sections and stuck together. She distributed the cake amongst friends and neighbours.

William Bycroft was head of the bakehouse and the cake expert, and invented the idea of making it easy for a bride to cut the wedding cake by pre-cutting a wedge and tying a ribbon round.

William Bycroft, Terry's baker 1922
(Courtesy Borthwick Institute)

Bycroft made the cake for the christening of Edward Prince of Wales, in July 1894. He took it to Windsor Castle himself and stayed for two weeks as a guest of the royal family. Thomas Terry allowed him a guinea a day expenses. When he retired in 1927, the secrets of his art were passed on to Peter Gee, who became chief baker and confectioner, and made the cake for the Duke of Kent's wedding in 1961.

In 1906, the range of Terry's boiled sugars was still growing. There was the 'very superior' list, including menthol, eucalyptus and pine tablets, cinnamon, greengage and butterscotch drops, mint rock, lime fruit squares and floral tablets, and the merely 'superior' list with its mint bulls' eyes, cachou squares, apricot and cherry drops, cyclists' refreshers, dogs and elephants, Havelock stars, cockle shells, crystallised 'coker nut' balls, Algerian fruits, lemon bullets, large Nelson balls, Indian corn drops, midget varieties, nectar drops, white pennets, ribston pippins, Scarborough shells, Togo bullets and Tom Thumb drops. Lozenges came in a variety of flavours, from fragrant cachous such as gelatine and violet, to throat hospital lozenges, gelatine packets, and silver smokers' cachous. There were others which carried a warning label. The packets read 'Poison, these lozenges contain belladonna' or '...contain opium'!

The menu for Terry's restaurant in St Helen's Square in 1900, offered the following:

Indian tea	5d
Russian tea	6d
Drinking chocolate	6d
Horlicks	6d
Buttered bath bun	6d
Welsh rarebit	1s
Scotch woodcock	1s
Gorgonzola cheese	6d

- Parfaits –

Strawberry temptation	2s
Harum Scarum	2s
Peach Delight	2s
Braised York ham	2s
Grilled Dover sole	3s
Chipped potatoes	4d
Jam or lemon curd tart	2d
Gentleman's relish sandwich	1s

Edwardian day trip from Terry's
(Courtesy Borthwick Institute)

By the early years of the 20th century, chocolate was becoming more and more popular. Terry's produced their first assortment called Britannia, and between 1902 and 1906 new products included York Milk Chocolates, Lion Mixtures, Duchess Creams, Empress Dessert, Diamond Mixture and Empire Mixture. The War Office Times and Naval Review of Christmas 1905 gave chocolate more status, calling it 'the sweetmeat of the Services...on marches, at manoeuvres, or any special occasion where staying power is needed'.

CHAPTER TWO

EARLY DAYS AND CLEMENTHORPE

In 1911 Noel Terry, son of Thomas Terry and grandson of Sir Joseph Terry, joined the family firm. In 1915 he married Kathleen Leetham, and his brother Joseph Edward Harold, known as Harold, married her sister Constance. Noel recalls the Terry connections with York.

We have records back to 1370. I think one of our main periods was when the Terrys were very well known as clockmakers, in the 1680s. I have a watch made by Reuben Terry. The clock at the Debtor's Prison is made by John Terry and was originally one handed.

We lived at Trentholme [on The Mount] and kept horses there. My father in law, Henry Ernest Leetham, and his family used to invade Coney Street every Saturday morning complete with Victoria and pair, and a car was not to be seen. In those days the ladies had very large hats and I remember an aunt of mine wearing a skirt which literally trailed on the footpath.

Ernest Leetham was the third son. Sidney was his brother, and they were very big in Leetham's Millers of York. Ernest was also a member of the Merchant Adventurers and Chairman of Terry's for a number of years. I would say our firm in those days was rather going through the doldrums and when he came into it, he added great life to the place and his connection is one I have never ceased to be thankful for. [Ernest Leetham was Chairman during the First World War, when Noel was away in the army].

I went to Terry's when I must have been 20. I'd been to a school in Filey to start off, and subsequently to Marlborough. I joined up when war came. I served in France, and I wasn't far off Thiepvale, very largely trench warfare in my time there. I have in mind two school friends, we used to see quite a lot of each other, and I was the only survivor.

My grandfather was Lord Mayor. Frank Terry was also a great man in the council, which I never was. We were in a growing business and I felt that all my duty was to my company. I served with Frank for many years. He was a step uncle but there were only 12 years difference between us. In our time, Terry's and Rowntree's were extremely good friends. The Rowntrees are a family for whom I have a very great respect. In my early days we were boiled sugar makers but we later developed considerably the chocolate side. But I wasn't much in favour of advertising, we were a small firm. Was there any good in whispering whilst other people were shouting?

Directors and senior staff, 1920s. Front row - Noel Terry is second left, Sir Francis is third left, HJ Wilkinson second from right. George Battrick is fourth from right in middle row
(Courtesy Borthwick Institute)

Noel's other grandfather was Edward Peart Brett, from Nottingham, who founded the York brewery, Brett Brothers. In 1896 he bought Trentholme, naming it after the River Trent. Later he transferred ownership to his daughter Sarah who had married Thomas Terry, and Noel and his siblings were brought up there. The house was later sold to the Leethams. Sidney Leetham owned the house opposite, Elm Bank. Colin Sheppard in his article in York Historian number 25, about Edward Brett, describes The Mount, where some of these families lived, as 'a fashionable residential area and wealthy enclave in the city'.

Len Smith spent all his working life at Terry's, starting out as an errand boy before the First World War. His wife Ethel recalls,

> He had a bicycle with a big basket. He used to go to an old lady down Clifton, every Saturday afternoon. She'd ring up and ask them to send a small brown loaf. And Miss Calvert, who was manageress, would feel sorry for him and two or three times she put fancy cakes in his basket.

> Eventually he had to go inside the shop and was a porter. Mr Wilkinson was a director of the firm, we called him HJ, he used to wear a Quaker hat, and Len would go to his house and do errands for his wife. He came home one day and said, "Do you know where I have to go to? Harding's for two pairs of ladies combinations. I daren't go, will you go with me?" So I went with him and bought two pairs of combinations. But they thought the world about him.

> I went to work at Terry's and I got friendly with Len. And he worked up in the jelly room and he'd come down into our place and get these jars to fill with calves' foot jelly. And there was only him and an old man in this place, and he said, "By gum Len, there's a grand bit of stuff come to work in the boiling shops. If I was younger, I'd be hanging my hat up there". Len didn't tell me that for years afterwards. He used to ride behind me, both on bikes, and then he got very bold and he says, "Will you go to the Empire tonight?" (It was Florrie Forde). So I says, "I'll have to ask my Grandma". And she said, "I like that lad, he's clean and a nice spoken young fellow. He'll be all right".

> Then he was made an overlooker. And when they built the big factory up on Bishopthorpe Road, he was in charge of the packing room. There was 300 girls in that one room. A lot of people didn't like him because he was too particular, and they daren't have a chocolate on the floor or a bit of paper or anything. One of my sister's girls went to work there and she'd got this hard Montelimar, and she said, "I was just nicely chewing it when Uncle Len came and he said, 'Miss Thompson, we have a department upstairs that tests all our chocolate, when there's a vacancy I'll let you know'." She laughed about it for years afterwards.

> Sir Francis came to see him two or three times. He'd bring him peaches and grapes from his own greenhouses. And he said, "I've known this young man since he was a little boy. And there never was a cleaner boy anywhere!" Len died when he was only 63 and he [Sir Francis] sent me a lovely letter and said if there was anything they could do for me, I had to tell him.

The workforce was growing, and in December 1913, an engineer at the firm earned £2, a cleaner 12s, a yard man £1.5s, and a joiner between £1.13s and £2. That year, Frank Terry went to Germany to look at methods of chocolate making. He returned with a refiner, triple mill, two pot conches and three melangeurs, all equipment needed to turn out chocolate of the highest quality.

Terry's Territorials had been formed early in the century, and in 1910 they included 13 privates, one sergeant, a lance corporal, company sergeant Thomas Milner and a drummer, who would soon be called upon to serve their country.

Territorials 1910, Walter Davy is first left on back row.
(Courtesy Walter Davy Jnr)

The First World War began in 1914. Rationing affected the confectionery industry like most others, and staff went off to join the forces or work in munitions factories. A whole generation of men were wiped out during the war and there were men who did not return to Terry's. Noel Terry came back but had been badly injured with shrapnel. In 1919, a new building was added to the Clementhorpe site. An agreement between Terry's and the trade unions dated 18th July, reduced hours of work from 49 ½ to 47, with six days holiday after service of twelve months, and three days holiday after service of six months. For overtime, men received time and a quarter for the first two hours and time and a half after that. Between twelve noon and midnight on Saturday, pay was time and a half and double time on Sundays. The three shifts were from 6am to 2pm, 2pm to 10pm, and 10pm to 6am. Men of 22 or over earned 55 shillings a week, but women aged 18 and over only earned 30 shillings. Piece work enabled workers to earn at least 25% above this.

Building of Clementhorpe extension
(Courtesy Borthwick Institute)

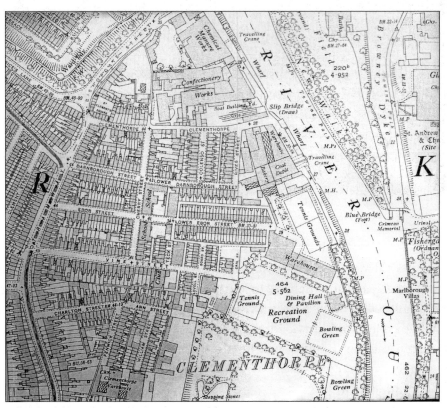

Map of Clementhorpe 1931
(Courtesy York City Archives)

Alice Leaf began working at Terry's in 1918 when she was 14 years old. During the war, when many of the workforce were serving overseas, some of their jobs were taken by women. Alice had been to a school in Clifton where the fees were a penny a week. This education ensured she had beautiful handwriting and an aptitude for figures.

A neighbour took me down to Terry's, Ada Winterburn. She was the timekeeper then, because the men were in the war. And we met Mr Milner, the factory foreman. I went into his office and I had to write something, then he said, "You're a clean, tidy girl, would you like to be in my office?" I worked in Clementhorpe, till I got married in 1926. I was very lucky. We got a holiday and we got a half day holiday for the races.

I did the wages for the packing room. It was piece work. And every box of chocolates they packed, they had to put a ticket in with their own number. We'd go and collect the work in the factory, bring them back to the office, count how many they'd done, enter it in the books and make a check out. At the end of the week, it was taken to the time office and they were paid through a little window.

We had an overall with long sleeves, and cuffs. And the only thing we used was a Ready Reckoner. If you couldn't reckon it up in your head, you'd look and see. I didn't type. We had a person there that used to take the letters, Ida Ede. We had nice desks and a fountain pen made for the job, 'cos we had to write through carbon. We had ledgers, a long narrow book where we put it all down. My wage was six shillings a week. It wouldn't go far today, would it?

I can remember them building the Bishopthorpe Road factory. We were the first ones to go to the offices. When you went up to the clock tower, there were no lifts. But you could see all round, it was lovely. I liked the smell of the cocoa beans, when they'd roast them.

We stayed dinner there, 'cos it was too far to go home. On Mondays, the fry up, they used to put it all in a dish, potatoes and vegetables and gravy and meat, and cover it over. And the boiler man would put it in the ovens and heat it. And we could buy waste, nine pence a pound of chocolates.

I was only allowed to go to Terry's dances with my sister Annie. I remember the Lancers. You had to have all your best underwear on because they'd lift you off your feet and swing you round. Some of the dances were quite energetic. I had to be in at nine o'clock every night, no buses, we had to walk home. When I was thinking of getting married, the boss called me in, Mr Milner, and he said, "Do you think you're doing the right thing?" You weren't allowed to work when you married. You had to finish. I felt a bit sad at first. And they collected quite a bit, the firm and then the girls collected. In fact they made my wedding cake, it was beautiful.

Office girls 1920.

Back L to R – Gladys?, Doris Adair, Emily Oliver, Doris Drew, Alice Stockdale. Front Dilys Smith, Alice Wales, Ivy Collins, ? Reid

(Courtesy Alice Leaf née Wales)

Another lady who worked for the firm in the 1920s was Sheila Elmer's mother, Lily Henderson, but she was at Terry's laundry. Sheila recalls,

Mother went to Terry's to put her name down and they accepted her and put her in the card box department, assembling boxes. They come in flat packs. She stuck it for two weeks and said she was bored stiff, 'cos she was a very lively character. So this friend said, "We've got a vacancy in the laundry". You went into Skeldergate and the other side of the building was next to T F Wood's warehouse. She used to chatter about the warehouse lads. There was only four of them. And the forewoman was called Mrs Hearne.

Anything that needed washing came down to the laundry. Tablecloths from Terry's café in St Helen's Square and the big white jackets that the directors wore, but when they were going round they would have big white overalls on. When she first started, they put mother on ironing, and the other two girls were doing the washing. The pretty little organdie type aprons and tops that the waitresses wore, they were terrible because they had to wash them, and they had to be dipped in cold water starch. It makes them very stiff, but when you're ironing them, it sets straightaway, so if you did not get those pleats absolutely perfect, you had to start all over again.

So again mother's nature, she did the ironing for a bit, then said to her friend, "I wish I could do the washing". And the friend was absolutely staggered but she jumped in quick and said, "Ooh yes, lovely". So mother switched over and got her hands up to her elbows in soapsuds, from half past seven to half past five. She stayed there until she married in the late 1920s. They had a very big bath that they soaked things in overnight if they were badly marked, and evidently these four ladies would take it in turns to have a lovely bath there. And they would drape down these sheets, as a sort of screen. When it was her turn and she was really enjoying being in the bath, she heard the door and a man's voice and was absolutely petrified. And it was one of the Terrys. She said, "I hardly dare move in case there was a ripple of water. But fortunately he didn't investigate".

There was a gentleman who was responsible for a lot of the stores, and mother talked about ginger coming in and eggs in isinglass. They were all stored in this warehouse. I think she must have been a bit of a daredevil because she extracted this egg for lunch. But the man came along so she had to hide it quickly [down her front] and he obviously knew what she was doing, so he gave her a great big squeeze. She didn't like to say a word but she knew where the egg was going. And one time, the men from the warehouse next door dared her to get in the crane that swings out over the river. I think they were all young people together so they were quite lively. And she swung out over the river and down into the boat. And this foreman shouted at her, he was quite cross and gave her a piece of his mind.

Terry's Office Staff c1920
(Courtesy Borthwick Institute)

She talked about going into Skeldergate and a little shop on the corner where they'd buy a pennorth of vegetables and cook their dinner on the stove. And she liked going dancing.

She got this flapper dress, low waisted, beaded all the way round. She thought it was beautiful. And she came downstairs and Great Aunt Minnie said in broad Yorkshire, "Get thissen back upstairs and put a cardie on, if Uncle Charlie sees you with bare arms!" But she loved dancing and she continued until she met my father and married.

Elsie Hall was the cook housekeeper for Noel Terry's sister, Frances, and her husband Lieutenant Alfred Hewitt, from the 1920s until 1937.

You wore a white apron and printed dress and cap, always. They had three children, two girls and a boy. You only had one half day off a week, and every other Sunday a half day. The rest of the time we were working!

I had to do the cooking and sorting things out. There was a kitchen maid, cook, parlour maid, housemaid, nursery maid, nurse, governess, and a sewing woman, and then a chauffeur and a gardener. I ordered all the food. They had breakfast, a proper lunch, afternoon tea, like scones and sometimes sandwiches and cake. Then dinner at seven o'clock. There would be soup, fish, meat, a sweet and a savoury, and sometimes grapefruit or an hors d'oeuvre before the soup. Just depending whether somebody real posh was coming. The savouries often used to be on a biscuit, like a cracker, with cheese and a sort of cream mixed in with it. And then we'd often do like a water lily, a hard boiled egg cut in little hearts, with little leaves of watercress. They'd finish off with fresh fruit, then coffee.

Lily Henderson c1920, aged 19.
(Courtesy Sheila Elmer)

Sir Francis and Lady Terry came a lot, and of course Noel Terry, and Mrs Hewitt's sister, Lady Baldwin. [Frances Hewitt's sister Kathleen Terry had married Air Marshal Sir John Baldwin who was aide-de-camp to King George V].

Football team and supporters 1920s
(Courtesy Borthwick Institute)

Joe Smith began work at Terry's at the age of 14 in 1924 and started off in the nougatine department at Clementhorpe.

Raymond Waller was foreman. Nougatines we'd send to the enrober room, and they used to cover them with chocolate. I'd twist the wheel on the machine that cut the shapes out of these nougatines. It didn't have a belt on it, it was hand driven. They'd boil it up on three or four fires, and Raymond would mix it in a basin on the fire. Then they put it on slabs to cool, and we put it through this machine and cut it up into shapes. As we were doing it, Ray was making another mixing, he'd tip it onto a slab, spread it out and cool it off.

We'd take it in a big tin, two off us on a morris board, with wheels under it to lift it up like a pallet. I did that for four or five years, then went into the Almond Paste room. It was warm in there, attached to the boiling shop, where they made all the boiled sweets. Every Saturday morning they swilled it all out. You had a little machine, and you put mixings in it, sugar and ground almonds, and flavouring, then cut it into shapes, then that went into the enrober room to be covered.

Clementhorpe was a proper old fashioned place, little departments all over the place. Old fashioned lifts, you'd pull a rope to set it going. We'd get flavours from a chap called Mr Gamble.

[In the depression it was] *very rare they laid people off, not like Rowntree's where they laid people off regularly. When I started, I got eleven shillings a week. It was a good firm to work for. At Skeldergate, they'd take a lot of stuff in from up the river. Bob Barron was in charge. They used to buy all the boxes at Waddington's from Leeds. When the river came up it would flood. You went up a slope to the five storey building at Clementhorpe. You could go in at the top end, when the bottom end was flooded. They didn't clock in, they'd have a medal on a board, and put it in a box, and somebody at the time office would take it in a sealed box, after half past seven. The foreman used to fetch a book out and it was written in this book.*

I used to crystallise ginger and cherries and make rum truffles. I enjoyed all my time at Terry's to be quite honest. It wasn't hard to go to work. I finished up as foreman in the raw material stores, where they took everything in, the sugar, flour, almonds. We only had five men. They'd make strawberry jam in the boiling shops. Wisbech, they got their strawberries from, and the girls used to come out of the packing rooms to pack it all. [The firm used a lot of raw materials. To make a quantity of nut chocolate, for example, they needed 14 kilos of nuts, four kilos of Carupano San Aroso cocoa beans, 16 kilos of sugar and 150 grams of vanilla. Filbert Kisses consisted of five pounds of sugar, five pounds of fondant, half a pound coffee essence, three pounds of roasted filberts, and one and a half pounds of dessicated coconut].

Sugar almonds making 1930s
(Courtesy Mike Grimes)

Cake wrapping 1920s
(Courtesy Mike Grimes)

It was all hand operated in the Clementhorpe days. Before they got overhead cranes it was all hand lifted, Dick Shears and little Bernard Pears used to do all that work.

Some of the rooms would have Christmas parties. There was supposed to be no alcohol, but they'd have cakes set up on the conveyors. And the maintenance staff used to go across for something to eat! After fifty years service, they sent you into town, somewhere in Spurrriergate you had your photograph taken. [These were displayed in the main gallery at the Bishopthorpe Road factory, where there were photographs of all staff who had completed 50 years. It was affectionately known as the Rogue's Gallery].

A number of members of Betty Metcalfe's family worked at the company.

My father's mother was left with a large family when her husband died. She was a very good needlewoman and she went as sewing maid at old Sir Joseph Terry's. They belonged to St Olave's Church.

My father worked there for 50 years. He was only the third person who had done so. My mother worked there during the '14-'18 war, in the samples department. Two aunts were overlookers. One cousin was the watchman, one worked in the chocolate mill, one worked in the pastilles, and later I worked in the wage office. Father was in the war but that counted as service. He worked at Clementhorpe most of his life in the sugar boiling department. And he made stripey mints, humbug mints, twisted barley sugar sticks and some very special rock which Terry's made, which was oval in shape, less than an inch wide, and less than half an inch thick. The outside was clear sugar usually lemon, or pink if it was raspberry. Right in the middle, in tiny letters, it said what the flavour was.

He was very proud of the fact that he was an expert in the field he was in. It was jolly hard work. He used to get some terrible scalds because there's nothing worse than hot sugar, which came out the consistency of treacle which they poured onto metal slabs covered in oil so that it didn't stick. And then it had to be worked while it was in that scalding state. He'd get terrible stings as well because you got wasps by the millions.

There was no air conditioning at Clementhorpe. It had been an 18th century brewery and that was where the boiling shops were. They built the tall five storey block which was where they actually prepared the very early stages of the chocolate.

My father was secretary of the fishing club, and belonged the football club in his younger days and played at the tennis club. Mother was only there the shortest time. She was in the sample department because she was tiny like me. They thought that was the best job for her, doing the silk bows on the bottles of sweets.

Football team c1914. Frank Metcalfe, father of Betty, first left on front row
(Courtesy Betty Metcalfe)

Auntie Grace had been overlooker over all these girls for years. I used to not know them by name, but that they were one of Auntie Grace's girls. And it's not many years since one of them stopped me and said, "Oh Betty, I remember you when Grace used to take you in a pram". They knew me from being a baby, when I had my little leather gaiters! Grace retired when she was only 51, gave up her job to nurse her sister with cancer because in those days you just battled on, on your own. She was strict but they absolutely worshipped her, 'cos they knew if they'd any problems, go to Auntie Grace and she'd help them to sort it out.

At this time the firm claimed to include 'a sufficient percentage of disabled ex-servicemen to place the name of the firm on the King's Roll'. There were also additional benefits for the workforce, such as a rest room, first aid attendants, and a welfare office in charge of cleanliness and hygiene.

In the early days of the factory, there existed a Suspension Book, recording the instances of staff being suspended. In the 1920s, this seemed to be very frequent. For example, in the month of August 1923, the reasons for suspension included being insolent (half a day), packing overweight (one day), interfering with the machine (three days), bad work (three days), bad packing (one day), and in April 1924, suspensions were given for striking a girl with a funnel (half a day), labelling boxes wrong (one week), wrong weighing (one week), leaving the room before the second bell rang (half a day), bad foiling (one and a half days), as well as 'left a handkerchief on hot steam pipe during dinner hour' (half a day). Of course these periods of suspension were unpaid so if someone was suspended for a week, it could cost them dearly. In early 1925, a man got suspended for five days for 'very bad piping' (on top of the chocolate). Another man got five days for 'bad tin foiling and packing', 'larking in the cellar' got half a day, and 'inattention to work' one and a half days. For reading a newspaper, someone got three and a half days, and the van driver who brought him the newspaper got three and a half days. In July of the same year, a suspension of four and a half days was the reward for 'larking with a pulley block' and one day's suspension for 'running down the yard with a bike'.

In December 1922, Mr H J Wilkinson, or HJ, the Managing Director, was presented with a morocco bound album to mark the completion of 50 years service with the House of Terry. It took place at the Vine Street packing shop, and was attended by representatives of all the sections of the firm, which testified to the popularity and esteem in which he was held. It was presented by Albert Jagger, the 'grand old man' of the firm, with signed photos of the staff and 550 cards. HJ had worked in the counting house, been appointed secretary to the company in 1898, then in 1903 he became director, and in 1904 managing director. He was very supportive of the social and sporting side, and instigated the Wilkinson Angling Cup as an annual competition. He was also very interested in natural history. The Botanical Garden owned by the Yorkshire Philosophical Society was under his entire care and he was honorary curator (botany) of the society for 27 years. During the First World War he was able to contribute seeds and plants of medicinal value for cultivation in order to meet the shortage caused by the stoppage of foreign supplies. He also felt that plants such as lavender and peppermint, when grown under favourable conditions, were greatly superior to those of foreign origin.

The directors gave a banquet in his honour at the De Grey Rooms in January 1923. A toast was proposed by Ernest Leetham, before a presentation was made. Mr John Lishman Varley said that three important dates should be remembered, 1767 when the firm was founded, 1872 when HJ joined and 1922 when both were still going strong. Presentations were also made to five others who had given 50 or more years of service. In fact Albert Jagger had given 62 years to the firm. HJ said that the company was thriving because of the spirit which imbued the employees who wanted to 'give of their best to the company and their fellow men'. It was a 'spirit of helpfulness and conscientious work'.

Angling club, c1900.
Back row L to R – J Petty, chairman, J Bristow, W Ogram, J Pratt, A Croft, Samuel Terry, president and son of Joseph Terry, C Hudson, E Clark, C Stead, A Ferrand.
Middle row – A Metcalfe, T Gossop, J Hall, G Peake, William Milner.
Front row – R Kendall, A Brown, T Musgrave, R Meek, H Vause.
(Courtesy Borthwick Institute)

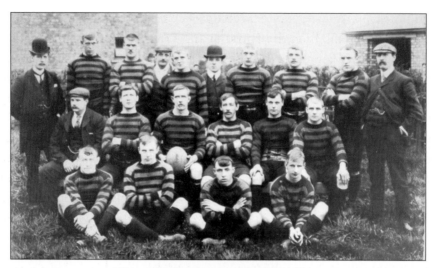

Terry's Rugby team, pre First World War
(Courtesy Borthwick Institute)

Dorothy Osbourne 1922
(Courtesy Borthwick Institute)

J Zimmermann 1922
(Courtesy Borthwick Institute)

Elsie Furby 1922.
(Courtesy Borthwick Institute)

The dinner consisted of boiled halibut and egg sauce, then roast beef with horseradish sauce or boiled mutton with caper sauce, steak and kidney pudding, rabbit pie, and vegetables. The sweet course provided plum pudding, apple tart, Yorkshire cheese cakes, jellies and blancmanges, with a final cheese course. The programme also included entertainment, with a song 'The Windmill' by Mr T Brinton, various glee songs in between speeches and toasts, songs 'The Farmer's Pride' by Mr C Donaldson, and 'Roses' by Mr P H Gatenby, and the final song, 'The Barber of Turin' by Mr H B Marston.

The 1920s was a busy decade for the company. From 1924, they had space at the annual Chocolate Exhibition, held first at the Royal Agricultural Hall and later Olympia, and before long they had developed new book keeping methods, and started a bonus scheme. In 1920 a five storey factory was built at Clementhorpe. But within a few years Terry's needed to expand again. In 1825, Britain's consumption of raw cocoa stood at 143 tons. A hundred years later, it was 56,000 tons. Terry's had outgrown the Clementhorpe works and found what it was looking for, land between Bishopthorpe Road and the racecourse. Today this site is an Area of Archaeological Importance. There is a well preserved medieval ridge and furrow to the south west and a Roman road from the south may have run through the site. There is also a possibility of occupation deposits or burials underground. Evidence of Roman settlement and cemeteries has been found nearby.

Work began on this site of 17 acres (out of 140 acres of cultivated land) in 1924, and the first phase consisted of a single storey factory, pump house, boiler house and attached transformer house, bean store and clock tower of 135 feet (which functioned as chimney and water tower, the supply system being pumped from the River Ouse). A year later the time office and general office block were built. The front office was designed on quite unusually palatial lines with a noble entrance hall and grand staircase leading to upper floors. The board rooms were spacious and lofty. The five storey block, completed by 1930, was 510 feet long and 80 feet high. The site was situated high above the river so that there was no danger of flooding, and surrounded by parks and woods as well as its own gardens. The time office was built in Baroque Revival style. The new buildings were said to 'reflect the very latest scientific conceptions of factory design and equipment'. They were designed by J E Wade, who had promised to make the site 'handsome and uncluttered'. The contractor for the works was Dorman Long of Middlesbrough, famous for the King George V Bridge over the Tyne, and also the Sydney Harbour Bridge! The Pennines, 45 miles away, could be seen from the roof of the factory. The combined area of the buildings was seven and a half acres, and together with three acres at Clementhorpe, and the cocoa store at Vine Street, the total usable area was over eleven acres.

Clementhorpe continued to exist, mostly as storage, but the C Mint lozenges and sugared almonds continued to be made there. Workers describe a 'battery of pans' used for making comfits, sugar boiling, preserving and crystallising the jellies. The refrigeration capacity was 12 tons daily, whereas the refrigeration plant at Bishopthorpe used 364 tons of ice per day.

The cocoa beans came originally from the Theobroma cacao tree, which had seed pods that would ripen and ferment, before being dried, washed and shipped abroad. The small trees only produced about five pounds of cocoa a year each. The basic beans came from West Africa, but the fine flavoured beans tended to be from South America, Samoa and the Caribbean.

When the beans arrived, they would go to the chocolate mill, where they were cleaned, roasted, then winnowed, (jets of air separated the shell from the centre of the bean), and gradually cooled. The taste of the chocolate which finally resulted came from the subtle palate of the chocolatier, who sampled the roasted and blended beans during the process, to make sure they were exactly right, for roasting is an art. At this stage the fragrant aroma began to appear. They were then taken to the nibbing machine, and put through rollers to separate the fat and melt it to oil. Fifty five per cent of the nib was cocoa butter. Some of the butter would go separately to be used for drinking chocolate. The nibs, now very small, were then ground to produce the cocoa mass, and sugar and chopped vanilla pods added. At this stage milk would be added to produce milk chocolate, though Terry's always specialised in plain chocolate. The brown glutinous liquid would then be refined on rollers to break down the sugar particles, producing at first a flaky powder, but more refining would result in a velvety texture. More cocoa butter would be added and the mixture put into the melangeurs (huge mixers). Next came the conching where the cocoa mass was stirred for many hours in heated pots. It was driven to and fro by heavy rollers in a series of waves, to produce a smooth cream. Moisture and any acid would evaporate. The cream was tempered, by cooling and more mixing, and for the first time it would be recognisable as chocolate. Then it would either be moulded into blocks or taken to the enrober room where it would cover the fillings, creams, toffees, caramels, nougats and fondants which came from the starch moulding department. Finally the chocolates were foiled, packaged and dispatched. It was during the late 1920s and 1930s, that the products for which Terry's became world famous, made their first appearance, the All Gold assortment, Devon Milk, Terry's Bitter Chocolate and Spartan. But it was the Chocolate Orange, created by Noel and Frank Terry, which was to prove the company's best known product over the next 80 years. And it was Noel and Frank who would take the company forward into a new chapter.

In November 1921 the press advertised the proposed rebuilding of the business premises at number 3 St Helen's Square and invited tenders. This would become the new Terry's restaurant, café, ballroom and front shop, which was a popular place for dances in the 1920s and '30s. But in 1924, the application for the renewal of the music and dancing licence was opposed by the nearby Harker's Hotel (at that time opposite Terry's), because of the 'nuisance caused by the syncopated and jazz bands engaged at dances at Messrs Terry's through the windows being open, thus preventing guests at the hotel from getting to sleep. When Terry's opened their new premises, everyone thought that it was their intention to use the premises for thé dansants, and not as a ballroom'. The licensee claimed that Terry's was affecting her health and brought several witnesses to attest to that fact, one of whom stated that 'almost every kind of musical instrument was being played simultaneously. People were dancing, shouting and stamping and trying to make as much noise as possible'. But Mr W Stewart, a barrister from Leeds, who was acting for Terry's, stated that 'jazz might not be music but a very large number of people like it'.

The magistrates agreed to renew the licence for Terry's but said that windows must be kept closed whilst music was being played and that after midnight music must be restricted to piano and string instruments. The complaints did not lead to any major changes on the part of the Terry's restaurant and ballroom. A musical evening, for example, in April 1929, had a 'panatrope' and records provided by John Gray & Sons of Coney Street. The music included 110 orchestral tunes, 10 organ, 8 violin, 9 piano tunes, four cello and 56 dance tunes such as the Mayfair Dance Orchestra, with 'I'm Crazy About You', 'Spread a Little Happiness' by Percival Mackey's Band, 'I Kiss Your Hand Madam' by Jack Hylton and 'Sally of my Dreams' by Jack Payne. An advertisement for the restaurant described the 'general style of interior decoration' as that of an '18th century English manor. The tearoom can be hired as a ballroom, with its special sprung floor. Lovers of the terpsichorean art will delight in its resiliency and the knowledge that they can dance until the early hours without that tired feeling which comes from solid floors'. The restaurant also had its second floor Oak Room, with walls finished in dark oak, and chamfered beams which created a Jacobean or late 16th century feeling.

Agnes Bridgewood was born in Scotland in 1908 and recalls going to dances at Terry's as a young woman.

> I was a member of the Caledonian Society, being a Scot, and they had supper dances in Terry's restaurant, probably every month during the winter. It was beautiful, all mahogany. It was 2/6d but it was subsidised by the society. They all wore dinner jackets and we had long dresses. We'd dance and then go down to the dining room for this beautiful supper.

The annual dinner of Terry's Cricket Club took place in November 1927 and guests were entertained with speeches, songs, pianoforte selections and an elocutionist. The six course meal consisted of -

Julienne or mulligatawny soup

Fried whiting and anchovy sauce

Chicken sauté and peas for entrée

Beef and horseradish sauce, or
pork, sprouts, braised celery, baked and boiled potatoes

Plum pudding and rum sauce

Cheese, celery and biscuits

Having done a tour of estates in South America at the end of the First World War, Frank and Noel Terry decided to buy a plantation in 1926 in Venezuela (from the Ruiz family) – the estates of Caruao, Bejorano and Santa Ana – which produced fine Criollo, cacao and coconut. The estates also included annexed lands of mountain, hill, meadows and waters for 650,000 bolivars, though they had to negotiate water rights. Criollo was said to be the best grade cocoa and continued to be used in later years, particularly in Terry's Bitter Chocolate. The company bought a launch called Sealark from an old shipyard at Shoreham by Sea for £225. It had been built in 1919, and was 30 foot long with a breadth of nine feet. The boat went via Leyland steamship Philadelphia to La Gaira, Venezuela, where it was used by workers who had to voyage upriver from the plantation.

The estate was developed later with the planting of more trees, improving the quality of the raw beans. The staff botanist Ernest Chambers went out to conduct business at the estate, and make reports to the directors, staying at the Miramar Hotel, Macuto, La Guaira. Before leaving he had to sign an affidavit before Noel Terry who was JP for the West Riding, to say he had no political involvement and was travelling purely as a cocoa buyer. To have its own plantation was a great boon for Terry's, and other companies followed suit.

Since 1984 the house named Goddards, on Tadcaster Road, has been a National Trust property, but it was built for Noel Goddard Terry in 1926, designed by Walter Brierley, the York architect known for his work on many York buildings, including

Terry's group in Venezuela
L to R – Frank (later Sir Francis) Terry,
E Matthes, Noel Terry, Ernest Chambers,
the Terry's botanist

(Courtesy Mike Grimes)

Workers at the plantation at Caruao,
Venezuela. 1930s.

(Courtesy Borthwick Institute)

schools. Noel bought more than three acres of land from Colonel Wilkinson of Dringhouses Manor in 1925, adding more land a year later. Goddards is described as 'an enchanting green oasis near York racecourse', the house being built in the Tudor Arts and Crafts style, with landscaped and wilderness gardens, naturalistic winding paths, terraces, rockery, cruciform lily pond, double herbaceous border, and a fine collection of shrubs, as well as a bowling green and tennis court. There were also spectacular rose beds, and a fragrant garden with mignonette, night scented stock, tobacco plants, rosemary and lavender. The area would be tended by six gardeners.

The garden was designed by George Dillistone of Tunbridge Wells. One of the attractions was that the factory could be viewed from Goddards, because of the seat placed below the terrace wall, though today the view is obscured by many trees. The project, carried out by Brierley and Dillistone, was compared with that of Gertrude Jekyll and Edwin Lutyens, where the garden complements the architecture of a house. The building firm of Thomas Anelay, well known in York, carried out the work. Unfortunately Brierley's health was deteriorating and he died before completion.

Noel Terry explains,

> *Brierley was a contemporary of my father's. He followed on, I think, in the same office as John Carr. He always had a great name and he was worthy of it. I think they knew the sort of size I was thinking of but the suggestions really came from them, which I passed with enthusiasm. Brierley's partner Rutherford played a great part. I believe he was responsible for the present chimneys which are certainly excellent.*

Noel's eldest son Peter Terry was born in 1919. He and his brother Kenneth as youngsters laid the foundation stone at Goddards and their initials are on the door. He also has other memories.

> *I remember going up to see all the scaffolding and builders there. I was about nine. We lived at 12 St George's Place before that, and I was at prep school at Scarborough. I was told to be jolly careful in the new house and not to play cricket in the corridors which I was inclined to do in our old home. I think we left there with one or two windows in the greenhouse broken by me, with a football.*

> *I had one disaster. I had a friend staying from prep school, and we turned the bath water on. It was above the drawing room with its marvellous ceiling and next door was the playroom. We forgot about the bath water and it was pouring through. Luckily for me, (I got into enough trouble as it was), the water came through into the room next door so we didn't spoil the ceiling.*

CHAPTER THREE

THE NEW FACTORY AND THE 1930s

From the 1890s when the industry was really growing, Terry's became a major employer in the city, especially for women. It was the beginning of a tradition as a 'family firm', not just the Terrys at its helm, but in its workforce. Many of them were from families who for generations worked for and were loyal to the Terry family and company. One of these was the Kendalls, Mike Race's ancestors. He explains,

Joseph Kendall of Warthill started as a confectioner's labourer in about 1875, and at least one member of each generation worked for Terry's in some capacity – as family nurse, housemaid, confectioner, baker, packer, engineer, until the closure of the site. My mother, Freda Kendall, was one of those – a factory girl in the 1930s and a married woman working 'to make ends meet' in the 1950s, when, after coming home from a 6 to 2 shift, prior to a 2 to 10 shift, she still had to cook, clean and care for an aging parent. Perhaps the unsung heroes of Terry's were its women workers. They were the engine room of the factory, making up the major part of the workforce. They worked much harder than most of the men, for half the wages. Without them and their quiet acceptance of their position, the chocolate industry in York would not have thrived as a major industry.

Another girl who joined Terry's at the age of 14 in 1925, despite being advised against it from all sides, was Elsie Banks (later Reed). She was one of the last young people to start at the old factory in Clementhorpe.

I left school at Easter and the first day after leaving I got rheumatic fever and for a week I was very ill. It left me with a bad heart. I got on my knees at the bedside and prayed that God would make me well so I could get work, as Mum was finding it so hard money-wise.

Elsie Banks (later Reed) 1920s
(Courtesy Lynne Townend)

A friend left school at the same time, Lily Doughty. She said, "Come up to Terry's", so I went every morning at eight o'clock to see if there were any vacancies. After three weeks I got offered a job, I think because I was tall.

The first day I started I had a packed lunch and I went to Rowntree's Park. I sat eating it and I thought it must be getting on for one o'clock. There wasn't a clock anywhere and in those days we couldn't afford watches. When I got back it was 1.30. They said, "What time is this? You'd better go home and come back tomorrow". My first wage was eleven shillings. My mum had ten shillings and I would maybe get a shilling back.

I always said I wouldn't go to a factory. I wanted to be a servant in a big house. But I went to Terry's and my sister Kitty came the year after me. People would say, "Women are always swearing and things like that", but they weren't like that, they were all really nice. I was in the enrober room for a while, I was on the scales, weighing the trays, which I really liked.

I was in charge of a machine. It was a lot of lifting and I was not supposed to lift with having a bad heart. But you don't take any notice, you had to work and that's it. I have not had a day off through my work so God does answer prayers.

Mr Milner was our boss. He had a son, he was great. Harold Meek used to be our foreman and Frank Wood another one, he was in the packing room. He'd stand at the end of the long tables with all the women working. I used to have a fancy for him but that's as far as it went.

In the enrober room, the machine would come by with different creams. You put them on a belt, it would go under the machine, get covered in chocolate, come out at the other end. I'd weigh them and they would go in the packing room. You put them on scales, and you knew straightaway how much, you got that used to doing it. Packers would come and help themselves off what they called gantries. I was a charge hand at the finish.

When I was 16, some of the girls I worked with and two or three girls from Rowntree's, formed a little group. Every Sunday we'd go walking the bridle paths.

We called ourselves the Orange Tam Brigade, 'cos we all had orange berets, so with rucksacks and walking sticks, we'd go to different places for the day. We'd really enjoy our walks, and have a picnic. We walked to Knaresborough but took a bus back, to Boston Spa, Kirkham Abbey, the White Horse. We hired a bell tent from the Army and Navy Stores in Fossgate and my Dad took us to a farm at Coxwold for a weekend and came and picked us up. We really enjoyed those Sundays, singing, 'I'm happy when I'm hiking'. There was no traffic in those days. I was 19 when I met my husband. He and his friends were in James Street choir. They'd go singing to different villages. I was at Terry's for ten years. I got married in 1935.

Packing department 1930s
(Courtesy Mike Grimes)

Once my brother Stan and Dad were coming along Tadcaster Road and a little pig fell out of a cart in front so Dad stopped and got it and it ran down Nelson's Lane. Dad informed the police but never heard anything, so it was ours. We called her Bessie. She had 19 piglets and one died. I was at Terry's at the time and it was the talk of the factory, 18 piglets.

During the National Strike in 1926, Terry's, like many other factories, closed completely for the few days that it lasted, but business was not much affected. Many new products were introduced in the 1930s. In 1931 Trent chocolates came in, along with Pandora, Delwood, Somerset and Avalon, and the 1767 box. More significantly, the All Gold chocolates were introduced and went on to become the company's major chocolate box assortment. What no-one envisaged at the time was that 60 years later the firm would be selling 7 million boxes a year. The following year, in 1932, what became the most popular of all the lines, the Chocolate Orange, was created at a cost of two shillings, although it actually started as a Chocolate Apple. At one time it was estimated that one in every ten Christmas stockings contained a Chocolate Orange. Between 1918 and 1938, trade at the firm doubled. Over the next few years, chocolate assortments Amazon, Bronze, Carousel, Criollo, Dahlia, Dee, Gold Leaf, Gold Ray, King George, Medway, Michoice, Poplar, Purple and Gold, Red Stripe, Royal, Severn, Sweet Thoughts, Thames, and Tradition all appeared, as well as Bridge Mints and Russian Caramels.

Staff await the Royal visit 1937.
(Courtesy Mike Grimes)

The highlight of the decade was the special visit in October 1937 of King George the VIth, and Queen Elizabeth, the Princess Royal and the Earl of Harewood, as well as the Home Secretary, Sir Samuel Hoare. According to the souvenir programme, three centuries had elapsed since a crowned monarch had officially visited York so it was a very proud day for the company. They toured the works and watched the processes of manufacturing of chocolate centres, covering, hand packing, manufacturing, cellophaning, foiling and machine wrapping, cartoning and dispatching, as well as displays of raw materials and laboratory testing. The royal couple seemed to be interested in working conditions and the welfare of the employees. A big banner and ribbons had been hung over the gates, and a marching band hired. Casket of chocolates were presented to the Queen, the Princess Royal and the two little princesses, Elizabeth and Margaret, who were not present.

Royal visit 1937, Queen Elizabeth presented with casket
(Courtesy Mike Grimes)

At the time of the visit there were 2343 staff at Bishopthorpe Road and Clementhorpe, 51 at St Helen's Square, 73 at reception, 11 at Middlethorpe Estate, 15 window dressers and 7 in the London office, totalling 2500 employees. Of these 492 were male, 1495 female. The heads of departments were – H Smith aged 43, Cream Starch, Harold Milner aged 28, Enrober, Len Smith aged 45, Packing, Miss M Morris aged 36, Wrapping, H Hatfield aged 34, Mill Room, Miss E Heppell aged 34, Cake Wrapping, and C Hardgrave aged 59, Despatch. The members of the Board were now Noel and Frank Terry, joint managing directors, (Frank was also chairman), George Stembridge, director and sales manager, Thomas Milner, director and works manager, and E R Dodd, the secretary.

Directors at Royal visit 1937. Front Right to Left, Sir Francis and Lady Terry, Noel and Kathleen Terry.
(Courtesy Mike Grimes)

Royal visit, women and caskets
(Courtesy Mike Grimes)

Dispatch department 1930s
(Courtesy Mike Grimes)

Because it was coronation year, the company produced a special King George Assortment, with 14 different centres, 12 of which were entirely new, including the Genoese with walnuts and cherries, the Rum Marzipan with pineapple and cherry, the Valencia Diamond, Muscatel and Marzipan Roll, the Cherry Delice, and the Apricot and Damson Sandwich. Additionally there was a new Coronation Assortment with 15 centres, including the Black Currant Trifle, Orange Strip, Almond, Cherry and Pistachio Genoese, and the Champagne Pineapple. The chocolates cost 10s for a 2lb box with padded lid, 5s for the one pound box and 2/6d for the half pound box. The publicity stated that the company had been 'famous during eight reigns – George III, George IV, William IV, Victoria, Edward VII, George V, Edward VIII and now George VI'. Other assortments could be bought with a special Coronation wrapper around them.

In 1936 an agreement was drawn up between Cadbury's, Fry's, Rowntree's and Terry's to agree on prices and conditions of sale. This was revised in 1940 and again in 1950.

Ernest Clayton, initially an engineering draughtsman, and later a chief engineer and then director, began his career with Terry's in the 1920s. He was involved in the design specification of the new factory, and some of his inventions were used on the production line, in particular devices for wrapping chocolates and boxes. His daughter Jacqueline Ake recalls,

Ernest Clayton 1908
(Courtesy Jacqueline Ake)

He was born in 1892 in Pocklington. He went to the village school, was very clever and was taken under the headmaster's wing but they couldn't afford to send him to the main school. So he left at 15 and went as an apprentice to Adams Hydraulics. He found he could earn more at the weekends cleaning his boss's car than he could at work. So he got some money from an aunt and virtually ran away to America and Canada in about 1910. He was in New York for some time, sometimes he slept under the bridges if he was poor, sometimes he had cheap digs where he used to put the bed's legs in tins of kerosene so the bedbugs wouldn't climb up. Sometimes he would send home for leather gloves and you can see pictures of him in a straw hat as a man about town. He also worked in Canada on the building of the Quebec Bridge.

He did a lot of pioneering engineering in those days, rode the trains to San Francisco, playing his mandolin in the guard's van or the freights. He'd play Italian songs and when Caruso was in New York staying at the Waldorf Astoria, Daddy used to stand on the pavement beneath, and listen to him practising his scales. He came back in 1921 qualified as a draughtsman engineer, with an introduction to a man at Rowntree's. And because he couldn't see the guy at Rowntree's, he went to see Sir Francis Terry who took an immediate liking to him. He went to work at Clementhorpe and then was instrumental in the move to Bishopthorpe. The front door was modelled on the Woolworth building in New York. I think he brought a lot of ideas back.

Jacqueline Ake as child 1950s
(Courtesy Jacqueline Ake)

He put air conditioning into Terry's. He also put it into Ben Johnson's 'cos it was very important there and into Cadbury's, all under the aegis of Terry's. He said that he brought in fork lift trucks and pallets, again an American idea. I don't know how popular it was in Britain at that time but Terry's was one of the first to use it. And wrapping the Neapolitans in cellophane. He has always said that he invented the 'tapability' of the Chocolate Orange. It took an engineer to make sure that it would, at the right tap, fall into segments.

Of course I got loads of chocolates as a child, even in the war when nobody else got them. He always said that if the Germans landed on the Knavesmire, he had the first plane out to America because he knew too much. He was very keen on Terry's Bitter chocolate, they had to be the right beans and it had to be the best chocolate in England. He went to America and Italy to get machinery. Then he became Works Director and had a secretary called Miss Swinn. She was with him for years and years, and had her own office and looked over the big typing pool.

I think he was in charge of the Terry's fire brigade. He got involved with the people. They had factories in Ireland and he went to Dublin. Then somebody who'd bought some chocolate said they'd found some metal in. So he went to Wrexham to defend Terry's. And he proved that the machinery he'd put in the plant would not let metal go through. And he won the case.

Terry's staff visiting Ireland. Ernest Clayton third from right.
(Courtesy Jacqueline Ake)

On Saturday mornings we'd go in and see the machines and these great big vats with molten chocolate in. And the refrigeration plant always smelt of ammonia. He'd wander round, in his job as Chief Engineer, checking that everything was going.

It was all very exciting going round the factory. Every year at Easter, I'd get an egg filled with rabbits and chickens. Sometimes at Christmas, I'd get a big chocolate elephant and a box of Neapolitans. If I liked orange ones, they'd be all orange. I'm still a chocoholic today. The directors' samples used to come round every month, All Gold was in a high class box then, the chocolates were different on both layers. He decided that it should be this high quality box of chocolates and should have all different centres.

At this time, Terry's offices had a central registry and all around it were the various sections, comprised of registration of orders, credit section, traffic section, sales ledger posting, sales analysis, invoice typing. At one side of the room was the section for the office manager, with the post room next door. On the opposite side was the safe. The firm used a new invention, the Sortergraf machine to sort its papers and cards, at the rate of 1500-2000 an hour. The Addressograph had metal plates for every customer and employee. The Folding Machine could fold letters at 7000 an hour.

Bill Godfrey was a representative at Terry's. He joined the firm at the age of 20 in 1935.

I wanted to go into the RAF but unfortunately I was colour-blind. I got the name of the sales director at Terry's. Dick Gossop was the office manager, and he opened the doors of the office and it was full of people at machines. The noise was terrific. They typed the ledgers, the invoices and the accounts, so it was quite a process. I worked in the office and wrote orders out. Then suddenly one day they said, "You're going out". Somebody was sick so I had to take the territory over. They recruited their sales staff to a large extent, by family. I was very lucky, when I arrived everybody said, "Who do you know?" There were such an amazing amount of types. Some were friendly, some weren't. One girl, she was from Queen Anne's, about 17 and very straight. In those days they did deportment, they used to practise carrying books on their heads. And a lovely smile she had, took my eye at once. It took me a little bit of time but we got engaged.

My first area, I went to Dundee. It was beautiful country. In those days we weren't salesmen, we were always referred to as reps. We had such a tremendous list, a terrific range of cake chocolate, and of boilings. We did things like calves' foot jelly. The place stank where they made it. It was supposed to be good for you.

We had an illustrated brochure. And as you went into a shop, your eyes were going all round and you were looking for something that was missing, so you could start the order off. You would go in talking pleasantries, anything to get started. But I had no training. I was just a clerk in the office, writing out orders but getting used to the prices.

We'd have about five or six hundred customers. Our main business was what we called CTNs, that was confectioners, tobacconists and newsagents. They were the hub of the trade. Then there were shops who sold boxes of chocolates. For wholesalers there was a lot of competition.

Mrs Godfrey 1930s
(Courtesy Bill Godfrey)

A good shop would take about a third of your list, would stock your boxes, your loose stuff and some of your cake chocolate. It's an amazing thing about the confectionery trade. It often depended on what happened years ago. If the mum used Fry's cocoa, the girl used Fry's cocoa. If you sold it to them, it would stick. All the time there's been this growing economic influence on the trade. The worse thing that ever happened was the supermarkets.

Dick Gossop
(Courtesy Borthwick Institute)

You got your bread and butter, lines that were fading and your new lines that you've got to push. The position you want is near the till. Somebody comes in for cigarettes and he sees something he recognises. And then there's the people who are susceptible to the next new line. And you go in and the shopkeeper's moved you away to the left or the right, so the new one goes in. You have to keep on bringing in something new and fresh. But Terry's didn't advertise. What we did was point of sale and window dressing. We had a team and they would go round, each area had a dresser.

I went as far as Aberdeen. part of Fife, had to go across the ferry, then St Andrew's, Perth, Pitlochry, up to Dunkell and Blair Atholl. I could park outside every shop. When I went to Dundee it was £5 a week, £3 a week expenses and a car. As a young man it was marvellous. And it was interesting. Every day you were meeting different people and different problems. Being very gentlemanly and polite to each other, given respect by your customers.

You were working for an elite firm, you tried to fit the pattern of being a gentleman, to be well dressed. At that time you'd have got the sack if you didn't wear a hat. I wore starched white collars and I often used to change at lunchtime, put a clean collar on. You develop a tremendous memory as a rep. With each customer, you remember whether they liked to talk about their son or daughter and they told you their troubles and what a hard life they had and you had to be bright, jolly, and smile. I was terribly shy but you became an actor. Funnily enough, a rep's job is very lonely. There's nobody you can turn to for encouragement, who can give you a pat on the back. It's just self-motivation. I've had my bag thrown out of the shop, I've been ordered out, I've been sworn at. You've got to be thick skinned.

In the early days, the orders were sent by rail in fibre light cases. It was so good that if I took an order in Dundee on the Monday, York would get it on the Tuesday and on the Wednesday I could see it coming out on horse drawn wagons.

Every Christmas we'd have a show. I held it in Dundee and they'd come in from various places and place a Christmas order. The big hotels had stock rooms and you'd set your show up. You'd get your big orders into the wholesalers and shops. And we always ran out. We could never make enough. It was amazing how these big boxes sold. There wasn't all the other things to spend money on. There were quite a few rich people about. In the days when I was courting my wife, she was off for a few days sick, so I took the opportunity to call at the house with a bunch of flowers and a box of chocolates. I was a go-getter in those days.

In 1935, All Gold Chocolates cost ten shillings for a two pound box, and five shillings for a one pound box. For the wealthier customers, there were the beautifully produced Velour Caskets which contained four pounds of Thistle assortment and cost £2. 4s, and the most expensive were the Silk Caskets with six and a quarter pounds of chocolates for £2.10s. They were often purchased for the boxes as much as the contents, and kept for years with treasured letters or photographs inside.

Of course most of the staff could not afford to buy the chocolates they produced. By 1937, the basic pay was 56 shillings a week for men, and 30/6d for women for a 47 hour week. The firm contributed to the employee sick club and ran a benevolent fund for needy cases, with free attendance at convalescent homes. A pension scheme had been introduced in 1931. Noel Terry received a certificate for presiding at the 12th Annual Festival of Confectioner's Benevolent Fund on February 19th. 'By his earnest advocacy, personal exertions and generous contributions of himself, friends and subscribers, £1658 was raised on behalf of the fund'. During the depression years, the firm offered a rebate to customers on their stocks of boiled sweets, which were reduced from 5d to 4d per quarter. It was discovered in the case of one shop that the sweets had been purchased nine years earlier and were still in perfect condition. They were made of pure cane sugar and packed in special bottles with a cork cap.

Irene McGouran began work in the factory in 1936.

I worked in fancy moulding, they'd do different shapes, they'd come down on a conveyor belt, we'd take 'em out, and put them in paper chutes and in a box. Most of the time we stood up. You got ten minutes break in a morning and afternoon. When you first start you can't believe your eyes when you see all these chocolates and you eat them till you get sick of seeing them, then you just don't bother any more.

We had overlookers who walked around seeing you were doing your job properly, they were very keen, and every Monday we'd have the nurse coming round, and she'd say, "Show me your nails". And see that you had your cap on, there was no hair coming out. And if you'd long nails, she'd cut them.

They had buses to come and pick you up, but when Terry's and Rowntree's used to leave, you couldn't get across the road. There was thousands of them.

They used to break down, the wrapping machines, and they'd bang and make you jump. You'd have to get an engineer out. When I was packing Neapolitans, that was piece work and they were all in wells, the different flavours, and you'd maybe nine of one, seven of another, five, four, or three. As you got used to it you just knew how many to pick up at one go. Fasten the box, send it down and the girl at the end would put cellophane on. Then I was on Chocolate Orange, they'd come down on a sheet, all the slices, and you'd put them in this mould, and they'd go on the conveyor and chocolate would go through the middle and that sealed them together. We used to get 'time and motion' round to make you go faster. For the Royal visit we all had to put clean overalls on, and caps, as if they wouldn't know you'd get chocolate on your clothes!

Terry's Amateur Dramatic Society was very active in this decade. In April 1937, three one act plays, 'The Cat and the Cherub', 'The Paths of Glory' and 'Goulash' were performed in the Pavilion, Vine Street. Noel Terry was the president of the society, and various members of staff took part both on stage and behind the scenes. Lily Heppell, the sister of local historian Syd Heppell, appeared in many of the productions. She was Hwah Kwee, servant of Hoo King, a rich merchant, in 'The Cat and the Cherub', which was an entry in the Drama League Competition that year. In November 1937, she played Clara Packer in 'Mystery at Greenfingers' by J B Priestley. This play was especially written for the News Chronicle Three Act Play Competition. Local firms obliged by lending furniture and other props for the productions, including Rentyorradioz of Gillygate 'for the loan of radiogramophone'! There may have been rivalry with the other chocolate factory, Rowntree's, but the Rowntree Players often helped with scenery for the plays, and once or twice they performed in the Pavilion. Terry's returned the compliment by taking part at the Rowntree's Theatre, in the East Riding County Final of the British Drama League Community Theatre Festival. The local press reviewer wrote that the players were 'establishing themselves as purveyors of excellent entertainment'. The leading man was often played by Harold Milner and the same writer, in his review of 'Winter Sunshine', stated, 'In his attempt to break away from being labelled forever as a portrayer of dude roles, Harold Milner finds the part of the blind man easier going than that of the famous actor in 'Bonnet over the Windmill'.' Other players mentioned were John Trench, Betty Freestone, Irene Berry, W James Richards, Gladys Birch, Douglas Coles, Kenneth Griffith, Eileen Ellison, Muriel Hudson, Molly Pearson, Elsie Senior, Walter Chadwick, Douglas Gosley and Jack Lawson. In a review of the play 'Pearly Pearls', a farce in two acts, the writer said that Harold Milner as the vicar 'lived the part' and 'one of the most amusing performances of the night was given by Lily Heppell as a cook'.

Terry's Amateur Dramatic Society, dancing girls 1937.

(Courtesy Joyce Heppell)

Terry's Amateur Dramatic Society. Mystery at Greenfingers. November 1937. Includes Peggy Craven, Lily Heppell, Muriel Hudson, Harold Milner and W Kendall.

(Courtesy Joyce Heppell)

Terry's Dramatic Society. The Cat and the Cherub. April 1936. East Yorkshire final of British Drama League Festival. Ernest Chambers is second from left as Wing Shee, W Kendall is second from right as Ching Fang, Harold Milner is third from left as Hoo King, and Lily Heppell is third from right as the male Kwal Kwee.

(Courtesy Joyce Heppell)

Alan Benson, who later became an engineer, worked on the Terry's farm as a schoolboy.

Where the caravan site is now, they called it Manor Farm. Terry's owned all the hilly fields, the fields immediately opposite Terry's, all the land right to Middlethorpe. There were the gardens and the piggery, the hens, they used to get all the eggs for the front shop. My pal at school, his father was bailiff. I always wanted to be a farmer and I'd spend time at the farm with Ken. And every season there was something happening, potato picking, turnips, chopping the tops off, all done by hand. If there were quiet times in the factory, and the production was low, they'd get the workers to whitewash down at Clementhorpe or send them to the farm to pick potatoes. We must have been on holiday and they said, "You and Ken can have a job if you want". So we picked potatoes for a week. And that was my first wage packet. Every weekend, of course it was horses and carts then, they'd take these carts that had been carrying manure up to one end of the cowhouse, take the horse off the shafts and tip the cart up. They had a very strong hose and they'd hose all the dirt off the cart. I wanted to do that one day and next thing I was going, "Fire", and squirting off in the field. There was such a shout. And I looked round and there's Sir Francis with his agent on two horses, shouting.

There were two cowmen that worked in the farm. And they lived in York. The cowhouse was fairly modern. They had troughs running at one end and a gangway at the side so they'd put the feed and cake in the troughs. At the end there were some big wooden boxes that they'd empty the sacks into, great big things with big lids. And I'd been cheeky with these two chaps. And they got hold of me and put me into one of these bins. I was enjoying this but then eventually, they left me in quite a long time and I was shouting, "Come on, let me out", but there was no answer, it was all very quiet. And I remember pushing this lid up and looking through and I thought, "They've left me". And I got panicky, I was only a 12 year old. But I got my shoulders under the lid and eventually lifted it up. And they'd put a ten stone bag of stuff on top. I got out but since then I've suffered with claustrophobia.

The land owned by Terry's also included fields which were used for cricket and soccer. The cricket square was apparently plagued by rabbits. There were cross country running races held there, such as the Yorkshire and North England Championships. Terry's motto when it came to sport and leisure was 'mens sana in corpora sanum' – 'A good worker is a healthy worker'. The company set up clubs for football, cricket, hockey, tennis, swimming, netball, angling, bowling, and even baseball. The firm donated £250 annually towards the sports clubs. In 1934, the Milner Trophy was presented to the Terry's Angling Club by Thomas Milner, for its annual competition. Over the next forty years, there were a number of winners, but members of the Duncanson family won the cup sixteen times.

Joe Smith recalls,

I played football and cricket for them. They had what they called Hospital Day, Frank Jones used to run it, down at Vine Street, and all the proceeds went to t'hospital. Vine Street was the main place for the lorries and wagons. There was showers down there, and their own bowling green and a nice pavilion. And they'd hold dances on a Saturday night, for a shilling. The pitch was past the factory up at Middlethorpe, and before that we were on the 'Mire [Knavesmire].

We played in the York and District, that was the team when they won the Junior Cup one year. That took some winning then, because all the junior teams in York and District used to go in for this. There used to be the York Senior Cup which is only about eight teams.

Joe says there was no difference between office, board room and factory when it came to sport.

They mixed to that extent. There was a big social life at Terry's. But you had to supply your gear yourself, they didn't supply anything, except the bats. Rowntrees were always in the first division, we never were.

Girls hockey team 1922
(Courtesy Borthwick Institute)

Hockey team 1936, winners hockey trophy, packing department.
Back Row – E R Dodd, D Audaer, P Carter, E Etherington, E Audaer, P Brown, J Hope, Len Smith.
Front row – D Heels, L Evans, G Stacey, E West, B Deighton.

(Courtesy Borthwick Institute)

Terry's vans
(Courtesy Mike Grimes)

Trip c1930. Back L to R - Sid Butler, Jim King, Joe Smith, Alf Coates. Seated – Harold Newbould, Arthur Gill, Frank Musgrave.

(Courtesy Joe Smith)

Football team 1934. Top Mr Milner, unknown, T Atkinson, Joe Smith, Harry Scott, Bob Collingwood, unknown (at end) Middle – Billy Eyeington, Ernie Mothersdale, Reg Bellamy, Ray Whaller, Alf Coates, Ted Irvine, Monty Lowther (trainer). Seated – Eric Sturdy, H. Newbold, Noel Terry, Lol Robinson, Ted Lickiss.

(Courtesy Joe Smith)

John Pratt was a confectioner in the 1930s. His grand-daughter Jenny Briggs explains.

He was there 50 years, and my father, George William Pratt, was there 46 years. He was an engineer. My mother was in the factory and a lot of the women used to wear their wedding ring around the neck. They always finished married women 'cos they weren't allowed to work. Nowadays there's married women in every job. My godfather was the Chief Engineer, Wilkinson. We always called him Uncle Will. If you mentioned my father, everybody would say, "Oh I remember little Georgie Pratt". My grandfather could have been on the gate when they clocked in, 'cos my father and my aunt used to say if they were late, he'd send them home. They were not allowed at work that morning.

Joan Pannett was 14 in 1934 and went straight to work at Terry's. Her sister Grace already worked there.

I remember the second day. I was in the packing room and Grace was on the next floor. Len Smith was the manager. I was feeding the belt and he came by and looked at me and he didn't look very happy. I wondered what I'd done wrong. I was working near the lift, and he opened the doors and went up. About two or three minutes after, he came through the double doors, stopped and looked me up and down. And I was very nervous. Then he went back up in the lift, came back, looked me over and went to talk to the overlooker. Then she beckoned me and asked me if I had a sister. And I said, "Yes I have a twin sister, she works on the next floor". She said, "He thought that you were going up in the lift as he was coming down the stairs". Just as if I'd dare do anything like that! She said, "I can't wait to tell him". I told my mum and she thought it was hilarious.

You never saw the office staff. They were real snooty. But I loved it there. There were some very nice girls. They had a belt training you to pack and I went on there and learnt. We had alleyways with seats. You had a big sack of straw shavings to put in the bottom of a box. You watched them until you learnt how to slip the brown cups off and put the chocolates in. You had glossy brown paper and that's what they put in the bottom of chocolate boxes. Now you get a corrugated piece. You did a layer of sweets, and some shavings and another layer. You was all brown with the dust on your white overall.

We got eleven shillings a week until you were old enough to earn your own money. We were on piece work. We got a penny halfpenny for a dozen boxes. And if it was warm weather, there'd be no air conditioning, they only had green blinds they'd put down outside the building, and by eleven o'clock they were sending you home. And sometimes you were off for three days. And you didn't get paid. At the end of the week, we all had to go to the Labour Exchange in Parliament Street, where there's a big toyshop on the corner. [The Disney store]. You had to queue for a pittance. You can imagine all the packing room queuing there.

Then I was asked if I would like to pack some export. There was about five of us. We'd do big tins to go to Australia, and different countries abroad. I remember I got three days' suspension once. You sat back to back, and often if there was a sweet missing out of your box, somebody would have one over. Somebody said, "Have you a cream…?" and instead of going round, I leant over and she put her hand out and Mr Smith was just passing and he gave me three days' suspension. He was a terror.

Frances Mercer was our representative for the union. But you'd no comeback. If Mr Smith said, "Suspension", you just walked home. The packing room was enormous, the length of that factory. I worked at the end nearest the racecourse. That was

Mr Smith's end and Mr Hayhoe was at the other. When my sister came in there, Mr Smith wouldn't let us sit together, he sent her right down to the other end.

If there wasn't enough packing to do, they had to find you a job in another room. And there was a vacancy in the enrober room, so I went up there. They had a tiny fork with thin prongs and I couldn't see their hands move, they were so quick, and all perfect marks they did on the top of chocolates. They were doing the same mark on all the sweets. They came down the chute, coffee creams and toffees, strawberry, lemon and limes. And I was sat there [doing it slowly], and the overlooker says, "Joan you're doing a lovely job but you'll never be rich with it". I said, "Ooh can't they go fast?" "Course they can, they've been doing it years. But they couldn't come and pack like you can."

Dorothy Cowan's father, Ernest Puckering, was chauffeur to Francis Terry from 1926. He got the job through rather unusual means. He was a taxi driver and one day,

He picked Sir Francis up for a fare, well he was Mr Frank then. When he got home there was a ten shilling note in the back. The only thing he could think of was Mr Frank, so he took it back. And he said, "Do you want a job, my man?" So he got a job and a house with it. I remember he had big long fronted Sunbeams. Sir Francis used to sit on the edge of the seat at the back and if me dad had to pull up sharp, he'd be almost on the floor. He got us a house in Balmoral Terrace. They lived in Old Nunthorpe, and it was easy walking distance. It was a big house in its old grounds, next door to the Ashcroft, and lovely gardens that went down to the river. Then he moved to Middlethorpe Manor. The Manor had big windows, and a lovely setting, but it would get flooded a bit. The Hall was turned into flats, and the top flat was where Joan Terry lived, Mr Frank's daughter, with her husband [Chedworth Gwynne who worked for the company – see later] and three children, Marcelle, Vivienne and Desmond. Eventually Marcelle married a property developer, Vivienne a wool

Children of Joan and Chedwyn Gwynne.
L to R – Marcelle, Vivienne, Desmond.

(Courtesy Dorothy Cowan)

merchant and Desmond was an accountant. Those three children were lovely kids but they weren't allowed sweets or cakes. Their nanny would bring them down, 'cos my mum used to make a chocolate cake, and they loved it. She'd bring them for a walk in the afternoon, to call and see 'Mrs Puck'.

Lady Terry [Sir Francis's wife] *was a very smart woman, she dressed beautifully. I remember Queen Elizabeth and George the VI came in 1937. I stood at the top of the lane and we were the only ones there when they went past, and we waved at them.*

Mr Frank used to go shooting a lot. We were very privileged children, because they'd go to Filey for a month or six weeks every year and take us with them. He took two cars did me dad, the groom took two horses, that's where I learned to ride on the sands. I wasn't allowed really, but the groom was exercising the horses and he'd rein in one and say, "Would you like a ride?" And he had

Ernest Puckering and Terry's car at Hopgrove 1912
(Courtesy Dorothy Cowan)

some old jodhpurs and he let me wear those. I was thrilled to bits. My dad would go up to Lord Middleton's and all over and the cars got filthy. He had to wash them down, clean the guns, wash mud off the boots, and next morning polish the cars and boots. He was a hard worker. When they were shooting, [the staff would] *get pheasants, partridges and the ends of the picnic baskets that were packed at the front shop, with lovely fruit loaves, apple pies and cheese. We were on holiday but me dad was still working. He'd have to come back to the gardens and get peaches to take back to the hotel. Terry's van used to take all our luggage. They only took my dad and the groom with them. When Robin and Joan* [Frank's two children] *got married, they kept the nanny on and she'd cook for them and my mother used to help out with dinner parties. They'd had twelve staff at Old Nunthorpe but the war took them away and they never replaced them. They had a head gardener, under gardener, my dad, and the groom. They had more land at Middlethorpe. We had a cottage there and we grew raspberries and brambles. A lot of those went down to*

Cottage at Middlethorpe. Home of Puckerings,
Francis Terry's chauffeur.

(Courtesy Dorothy Cowan)

the front shop in St Helen's Square. There was a market garden, that supplied the shop and restaurant and a farm at Bustardthorpe. The family were very kind. But when you live on the premises, you're never off duty. Sir Francis called him out one night, he had to go down into the cellar and my dad fell down some stone steps and broke his leg so that upset the applecart. It was quite some time before he recovered. We didn't have a lot of money but we had rent and rates free. When my dad died in 1953, they let us live there until about 1958.

Evelyn Hudson's father, Thomas Mortimer, husband Geoff and father in law Ben Hudson, all worked for Terry's. Evelyn explains,

My dad loved his life at Terry's. He was in the garage, a fitter, mechanic, and relief driver. Terry's were very self sufficient, everything was done at the garage, the wagons, the trucks, the reps' cars, the staff cars, the directors' cars.

He used to tell stories about the drivers. They got expenses if they'd got to stay overnight anywhere. And one of them used to brag he never paid for his bed and breakfast because he always had a bag of chocolate under his seat to pay for his digs. They'd go dog racing and stock car racing when they were staying away. It must have been in the days when they had to have a mate on the wagons, and they'd gone to Belle Vue at Manchester, stock car racing, came home with a stock car in the back of the wagon, they'd bought it! And they spent hours in the garage trying to do it up, but I don't think it ever did go.

When Sir Francis was knighted in 1936, they put all the works numbers in a big drum, and twelve were picked to go to London with him, for the weekend. And my dad was one of the lucky ones, they had a marvellous weekend, stayed at the Savoy and went to Drury Lane on Saturday night to see a show. Peter Terry [Noel's son] started like they all did, had to work through the factory, on his uncle's instructions, because Francis was the head, and Noel took over after Frank died. Peter was the same age as my husband Geoff, and they played cricket together for Terry's. Peter was good, he went to play for Yorkshire Gentlemen. We had days out at Reckitt's at Hull. There would be a football match, cricket match, a swimming gala, or a tennis match. We'd go in a coach and spend all day, you got your lunch and your tea.

My dad was a Scotsman, he had four brothers that loved to visit us in York. And Uncle John, when it got to about ten minutes to twelve, he'd say, "I'll be back in a minute", and he'd go and stand at the end of Richardson Street, fascinated, watching the Terry's lasses and lads leaving on their bikes, four abreast some of them, they had to dodge the tram lines, 'cos if they got stuck in the tram lines they came off. And of course if me dad got to know there was anyone leaving the factory on a Friday night to get married, there was always a decorated cart or a car towed it, [the bike] but nine times out of ten their work mates pulled it all the way up Bishopthorpe Road decorated with balloons and streamers.

Ben Hudson 1920
(Courtesy Evelyn Hudson)

When the war finished and they came back to Terry's, the lanyard in the flag pole had rotted, 'cos there hadn't been any flags flying, and they wanted a volunteer to climb the flagpole, and put a new lanyard in, and Geoff says, "I'll do it". The only ladder they could find was four foot short, so he scrambled the rest of the way up with his hands and knees, to thread the lanyard through. He ruined his overalls, his trousers, his boots, but he got a book of clothing coupons for doing it! And they used to sneak up there as well with binoculars when York Races were on! He was quite proud of that.

We've had some happy times. The market garden at Middlethorpe was run by Mr Elliott. His three lads and Geoff were all at school together, and any of my birthdays or our anniversaries he'd go and see Mr Elliott and bring a beautiful bouquet of carnations or chrysanthemums from the market garden.

The milk, cream and eggs served in Terry's restaurant were all from their own farm, and most of the fruit and vegetables were also grown there. An advert in 1936 for the St Helen's Square premises, read -

One of the favourites at the restaurant was the Exhibition Gold Medal Teacake. The original 1935 recipe was as follows -

Ingredients – 3½ lbs flour, ¾ oz salt, 6 ozs fat, 8 ozs sugar, 3 ozs yeast, 1½ pints milk, 12 ozs currants. Mix with 1¼ pints liqueur, 2 ozs sugar, ½lb flour, 3 ozs yeast.

Mix, stand 30 mins, scale and mould, lie 10 mins, mould again, lie 5 mins, pin out and tin, bake at 480-500.

The 1930s was the heyday for confectionery nationally and Terry's raised the standard. Sales of chocolate rose from 2,332 tons in 1925 to 4,836 in 1939. In this decade Terry's produced its Chocolate Orange and All Gold, and Rowntree's produced Black Magic, Kitkat, Aero, Dairy Box and Smarties. Cadbury's had launched their Flake in 1920 and Crunchie in 1929. Although all these companies continued to produce and perfect new lines, never again would chocolate be so new and exciting.

CHAPTER FOUR

WARTIME

Even before the Second World War began in 1939, the government was preparing for possible war. Two years earlier, Terry's had sent staff on courses about air raids and gas masks. On 26th September 1938, the territorials, including a number of Terry's staff, were called up, 'on account of the European crisis, with the German occupation of the Suedeten territory'. In July 1939, air raid shelters were being built. Vine Street had a pre-cast concrete unit for a shelter for 50 people, at a cost of £150. There was a shelter in the 'old chocolate cellar' at Clementhorpe for 170, at a cost of £95. Bishopthorpe Road had a tunnel shelter for 600, and a ground floor shelter for 1000, costing £1600. Sandbags were purchased, and steel shutters cost the firm £3000.

A hot water pipe system was used to heat the shelters, and 3" pipes suspended seven feet from the floor. A calorifier and pump from the new pastille stoves under construction were borrowed 'for the duration of the war'.

At the end of August 1939, Noel Terry's elder brother Harold died at the age of 53, just before the beginning of the war. He had served in the Artists' Rifles in the First World War. After attending Pembroke College, Cambridge, where he was stage manager for the Footlights Club, he was taken on as an apprentice journalist with the Daily Mirror, before becoming a playwright. His first play was 'Old Rowley the King', and after that he was commissioned by the Yorkshire Herald to write a serial story. This eventually became a novel about Dick Turpin, entitled 'A Fool to Fame', which was acclaimed by the Times reviewer, amongst others. He continued to write plays and was also an amateur actor, taking part in the York Pageant of 1911, as King Harold in the Battle of Stamford Bridge. He also appeared in the York Operatic Amateurs' productions of Iolanthe, and Amadeus in 1909. In 1921 his play 'The Fulfilling of the Law' was performed at the Garrick, and went on tour with the actress Constance Collier. According to Colin Sheppard, in his article on Edward

Peart Brett, who was related to the Terry family, (see Bibliography), Harold Terry's most famous play was 'The Man who Stayed at Home', which placed him at the forefront of the British dramatists of the day.

In September 1939, a few days after war was declared, female staff were encouraged to sign up as auxiliary nurses. There were classes held at the wages office, and the firm provided the text books. Air raid drill began, with the intermittent ringing of time bells and the extinguishing of lights in working rooms. On the 3rd November, the company announced that 'Public speech and music equipment' were to be installed in the control room of the five storey factory, with loudspeakers in each of the four tunnels and air raid shelter rooms. The system included an 'amp and record player unit, microphone, 12 speakers and necessary cable', and together with labour, this cost £54.4s.

A list of ARP (Air Raid Precautions) activities at the factory consisted of –

Decontamination and Anti-gas, Cleansing Station, Rescue, Messenger and Telephonists, Aircraft Spotters, First Aid, Stretcher Bearers, Fire Watchers, Shelter Wardens and Section Leaders. The Rescue and Decontamination vans were situated near the Time Office. Additionally the company had its own fire brigade.

Of course, the war brought rationing back. Chivers the jam making firm moved into Clementhorpe, and stayed there until the 1950s. The restaurant managed to continue and the factory still made a certain amount of chocolate. Before the war, the average consumption of confectionery had been 6¼ ounces per person, and this fell to 2 ounces per person per week, increasing in August 1942 to 3 ounces. In 1942 the annual allocation of cocoa was 1761 tons. The company sold 4,836 tons of chocolate just before the war, which went down to 3,627 in 1942, and in 1948, the amount was only 2,977 tons.

Many members of staff left Terry's to join the forces. The army regiments included the Duke of Wellington's, the Green Howards, the Royal Artillery, the Royal Scotch Fusiliers, Royal Armoured Corps, Auxiliary Military Pioneer Corps, the Royal Engineers, 11th West Yorkshires, 51st Anti Tank Battery, 54th Searchlight Battery, as well as the Royal Air Force, Royal Navy, Merchant Navy, Ministry of Works and Planning, and the Handley Page Aircraft Works.

In 1941 the lease held by Terry's since 1927 on part of the De Grey Rooms, expired. The building had been used mainly for extra offices. But in September 1939, it was requisitioned by the military. The ATS did their physical training there twice a week in 1940, whilst in June of that year, the Post Office telephone authorities took over part of the premises. In the 1930s, the De Grey Rooms had also been used for social events, including the Terry's Tennis Club and Swimming Club supper dances. Percy Barton of Barton's Catering had put a 'dancing floor' in there in October 1927.

Betty Metcalfe started work at Terry's in 1939.

I was at Queen Anne's until I was 16. They didn't entertain anybody in the offices unless they'd been to grammar school. I worked from half past seven to five o'clock for the princely sum of nineteen and sixpence a week, less national insurance. You stayed a junior until you reached 21.

I worked in wages, under somebody known throughout the factory as 'Cut Price Joe' because he set all the bonus systems and the piece-work prices. He'd go out with his clipboard and stop watch, and time the girls packing the chocolates or wrapping them in foil. He'd time a slow one, a medium paced worker and a quick one. So they had him taped, the quick ones used to work slower to affect the price, and then they worked like fury.

Betty Metcalfe 2005
(Courtesy Mike Race)

When I'd go round the factory, he'd tell me how long I should be, and then time me. Mind you, I was as cute as he was. We weren't allowed to speak when he was in the office and if you got too friendly with your next door neighbour he'd move you. We were on big desks with two drawers and a chair, all down the office in two rows and he'd sit at the front and look at us.

He had a famous black book in which he put down remarks about us every day. He thought we didn't know, he had a screw that he'd screw in the bottom of the desk so that you couldn't open it. Well immediately he went out, we used to unscrew it. He'd put down that you'd been too long in the cloakroom or done something you shouldn't have done. It was like a game of cat and mouse and the cat didn't win too often. Can you imagine that these days? They'd be on strike and taking him to court and heaven knows what.

Front entrance 1930s
(Courtesy Mike Grimes)

I had another job which was stores control, which took me every day round the whole factory including Clementhorpe and Bishopthorpe Road. Then in an afternoon I became a wage clerk. At Clementhorpe, Chivers took over what had been the boiling shops and father was head of that outfit. When the war finished, he came up to the five storey at Bishopthorpe and worked on something that was called a Difrano, a machine which put the colour of juice into cherries and pineapple.

Sugar got very scarce and cocoa beans were hardly imported. They did go on making boiled sweets, and barley sugar drops packed in tins. They went onto the inflatables and rescue ships that the aircraft and the navy had, as survival rations. They made Empire Chocolate, a universal thing with any cocoa beans that they still had in stock or they made vitaminised chocolate for army rations. I'd see these big troughs of things that looked rather like Plaster of Paris. And that was the vitamins in the chocolate. What had been a dozen different assortments were cut down to only a few. It was not until 1956 that the range grew big again. And it wasn't until after the war that Terry's ever made any milk chocolate.

The men could volunteer to fire-watch and females used to man the telephones at the weekend. And we had the doubtful pleasure of putting the siren on when we got the red signal, on top of the five storey block. It was an electric one, you just pressed the button and it started wailing away. We had some warnings during the daytime and everybody had to rush to the shelters but if you were on a fire-watch rota, you weren't allowed to, you had to patrol the office block.

We were all issued with steel helmets. Well me in a steel helmet was a sight to behold because they weren't like the army ones with a strap on the back, they were much deeper and had a wide brim. And I could literally go walking along the corridor, turn a corner and my hat went straight on. It was hilarious. In the afternoon, they had 'Music while you work' and all the girls in the packing room and the covering and piping and whirling rooms were allowed to sing, all the popular songs. It used to be lovely to hear all these girls singing together.

When the Blitz was on in London, we took over work for a very famous chocolate firm, Charbonnel and Walker's. Terry's made the chocolates and we had to do all the wages for it. We were allowed to have a pound of chocolates a month. We got some waste chocolates, over and above our ration.

We did have an adding machine in our office. It worked on springs of all things. It was very square, tinplate, with loads of keys. It was extremely hard, working on that all day. We were a long time before we got mechanised. We did have a typewriter and telephones. One of the typewriter companies would come and maintain the machines about every six months. When they discovered that we'd got this one, they asked if they could have it back for their museum. We had round rulers still, like in Dickens. Scrooge and his lot. They were made I think of teak, and we had plain ink in inkwells.

During the war we had great savings schemes. That was another of my jobs, Saturday morning, going round the factory selling national savings stamps and certificates, alternating with collecting for the Red Cross. They were extremely generous, except for the engineering staff who earned the most money. And it was like getting blood out of a stone. Then we persuaded people in the factory to knit for the troops, scarves and gloves and balaclava helmets, and socks. We had sales at the shop in St Helen's Square, made quite a bit of money for the Red Cross. We had War Weapons Weeks when the army would come round visiting with two or three tanks.

In fact Terry's Savings Group received a certificate of honour for special achievement during Wings for Victory National Savings Campaign in 1943. The company made many investments in National War Bonds during the war and into the 1950s. In May 1941, during 'York War Weapons Week', the city's target was £1 million, and they actually sold bonds worth £2,118,574. In June 1944, York held a 'Salute the Soldier Week', when £50,000 worth of war bonds were bought, and staff sent in £21.15s.9d

Office 1930s
(Courtesy Mike Grimes)

towards army charities. During the course of the week, Terry's restaurant gave free coffee to members of the WVS who were helping with the administration of the event. The last of these fundraising events took place in October 1945, when Terry's purchased £25,000 worth of bonds during York's 'Thanksgiving Week'.

Betty continues,

Then along came the aircraft people, Hill's, who made laminated aeroplane blades [for Jablo propellers], and repaired them. The smell was appalling, like concentrated nail varnish. They made this very heavy laminated wood. They used to bring RAF low loaders up Bishopthorpe Road to the factory with blades in various states of brokenness.

I was there when a plane crashed on Nunthorpe estates. Our office was on the Bishopthorpe side. We knew the planes were going out, then we heard this tremendous crash and the next thing we knew, the sky was full of debris. They were picking it up from Bustardthorpe allotments for days afterwards. And our boss went to the other side of the building and we decided to trail after him. We saw some of the airmen coming down in parachutes. There were machine gun bullets whizzing all over, right past Terry's. And we waited until it quietened down 'cos it was time for us to go home. We just got outside onto the back of the office block and the petrol tanks of the plane went up. Well I've never heard anything like it. It was horrifying. There were some Italian prisoners of war who were passing by at the time, because they used to go from the camp on Knavesmire into town and do things like snow shovelling and odd jobs like that, under guard. And some of them rushed to help.

There was an anti aircraft battery there and the barrage balloon in the garden at Vine Street. But what good one barrage balloon was, I don't know.

In fact during the war, the Terry's clock tower was used to keep a watch on the prisoners of war based on the racecourse.

Aerial view of Terry's during Second World War, with POW camp on Knavesmire
(Courtesy Mike Grimes)

Tank at Hill's during Second World War
(Courtesy Mike Grimes)

Winnie Mothersdale remembers working there during the war.

Hill's from Manchester came and took so much of Terry's over. Six of us went to Trafford Park to train. There was another girl and myself did our job and then two more did another stage and two more another stage. Quite a lot came from Manchester and lodged in York.

Cissie Colley also recalls the department.

There was no windows and we were painting aeroplane blades. It had to be a certain amount of varnish on, and if you got more, you had to scrape it off. We were so tired. You'd to go seven days a week, if they wanted you on a Sunday you had to go in. They dropped all the rules and regulations about labour, there was no bank holidays. It was terribly important 'cos they were losing a lot of aeroplanes. Three times I got dermatitis with the paint, and the doctor kept giving me cream. It was very hot in that place. It was hard, hot and heavy.

Then Cissie was moved up into the chocolate mill, originally a male only preserve.

There was three men and three women and we'd do shift work. They never let women do nights, just the men. You had to shovel wet chocolate over a right big roller. Then they poured it out into real deep tins. A man and a girl had to carry that to another shed while it got cool. It was bitter chocolate for soldiers, emergency rations.

When Elsie Hall came back to York, she went to work in the restaurant.

They were advertising for women cooks, because the men were going to the war, and they wanted three of us, and they put me in as the head one. They did have a chef who'd retired before the war, and they brought him in as an overlooker. This was June 1940. I stayed until January 1946, when the first men came back.

During the war, they couldn't charge any more than five shillings for a three course meal. There was always soup, and nearly always a roast of some kind, and fish. They served lunch from twelve o'clock to half past two. And then after that you could have salads or something on toast or sandwiches and cakes.

There was no problem with vegetables and we'd get spam. And salmon at times and sometimes lobster from the fishmongers. You'd make fish cakes and chips or, to make your meat go further, mix it with vegetables and potato.

They were really big kitchens, with ovens and little hot plates and a big grill. And there was a room where you'd prepare stuff. And a big walk-in fridge. Then another that we kept the fresh fish in, that always had ice. Downstairs was the shop, and the main restaurant was on the ground floor, and then there was another one upstairs.

There was a basement down below, which was the ladies' toilets, and there was a washroom, and when we fire-watched we had to sleep in the ladies' cloakroom.

For fire watching at St Helen's, there was an observation post and guard rails on the roof, with an alarm bell, telephone and ARP equipment. A steel scaffold bridge between the roofs of Yorkshire Insurance and Terry's cost £36 to build.

On the night of 28th April 1942, when York was badly bombed, in the Baedeker Raid, Elsie was not on duty.

I wouldn't volunteer because I'd had a funny night [the previous night]. We'd go to bed about ten, get washed and changed, and sleep in our slacks, in case anything happened. And the others were all fast asleep. It would be about midnight, I heard footsteps in the room, and knowing that there was supposed to be a ghost, I daren't do anything. We had four basket chairs where we used to sit. Then I heard a chair creak, and I was scared stiff. Then I felt the footsteps, they'd gone back onto this chair, and I never heard them actually go out. At six o'clock next morning I asked the night watchman if he'd been in, and he hadn't. So I said, "What about the cat?" "No, the cat was with me all night". So when it came to that night [the 28th], I didn't volunteer. And I thought afterwards it was a sort of warning. It was supposed to be the Grey Lady who walks to the Theatre.

Sometimes there was dances on where they were serving a meal later, or hunt dances where they had a breakfast before they went home. And the waitresses would pop into the cloakroom for a few minutes, and lie on one of the forms, and a few of them have said they felt a skirt swish past them.

On the night of the Blitz, there were only two fire-watching, and they put an incendiary bomb out. And then afterwards the two that were on, and the night watchman, they all got ten pounds each, which was a lot of money then.

Evelyn Hudson 2005
(Courtesy Mike Race)

Evelyn Hudson recalls going into the city centre the morning after the raid.

I worked at Kathleen Benson's [hairdresser in St Helen's Square]. *We had no gas, electricity or water. But Terry's restaurant had. The kitchen staff were very good, coming out with trays of tea and coffee for firemen, police and other workers.*

Elsie Hall remembers another air raid.

When the gas-works was bombed we couldn't have the same amount of gas, we had to have Calor gas. So we couldn't always use all the ovens, and I had to go down to the factory, to go and bake some game pies, because they had one oven, an electric one, that they used for doing roasted nuts.

We didn't get a lot of eggs, we got dried egg. In fact I showed Sir Francis how to do omelettes with it. Then he came back another day to see it again! He didn't come anymore after that, so he must have learnt! You couldn't always get ham so we'd put spam into hot water, and serve it with a sauce, or we'd make ham and potato cakes or spam fritters. And for fat for the chips, we'd sometimes use cocoa butter from the factory.

When I gave my notice in, Mr Gill, who was the manager at the time, he was a bit upset, and he said he didn't want me to go, and there would always be a place for me there. But how he would have done it I don't know because the men would be going back.

Elsie even cooked for the Princess Royal, who visited the restaurant during the war and had a meal in the Oak Room.

Betty Hartas joined the company in January 1944 at the age of 14.

I started in the Raw Materials, clerking, and I was only there a few weeks when they were short of staff in the bakehouse. So I spent some time there, just taking buns out of trays and stacking them. I transferred to the Raw Materials stores and was responsible for going round the factory each morning and taking orders from the managers.

They didn't have a canteen as such but for under 18s, there was a little hut on the water side near the time office block. And Mrs Broughton from Vine Street would come along and make national cocoa. And we could buy it at a penny a cup. It wasn't very nice but we were glad of it, being at work at half past seven. At the time office entrance, there was a metal roller that would fit right across. And dead on half past seven, Bert Woodburn, who was in charge, would pull a pin out and it would slot straight down. If you were in the way, you moved quick. But you daren't be late, if you didn't get in, you went back home. And the time office flooded of course. At one time, Cheddy Gwynne waded in there and opened the safe to get the stuff out, all the valuables.

He was a character. He was in charge of sales. And one of the reps had long hair and he'd told him to get it cut and he hadn't, so Cheddy walked him into a barber's shop, and told the barber to cut his hair.

When I was in Jam Dispatch at Clementhorpe, I was checking the wagons. They'd bring in the wooden crates, with 24 one pound jars or 12 two pound jars. And they fastened a label with the name and address on it. And when they came back out, I had to take these off and count them up and credit the companies with whatever had been returned.

The boilers were at the bottom of the yard and there was two huge doors and the firemen had to shovel coal in there. At a certain time, they were all shovelled out, red hot, onto barrows, and wheeled outside into a little part that was fastened off. And when it was cold, all the residents round Clementhorpe would come and collect the clinkers for their fires. Because coal was still rationed, so they used to always be in there scraping and scratting to get cinders.

Not everyone enjoyed the work at Terry's. Doreen Varrie

Started at Terry's in 1939, straight after school. It was dreadful in the pastille room where they sugared the pastilles and they all stuck together, and we had to separate them. They used to put them in great big vats. They were gums when they went in, and pastilles when they came out, but all the sugar used to stick... horrible! And on your shoes. They provided us with rubber gloves, but they were enormous, you couldn't work very well with them, so quite often the girls took them off, they were all sticky with syrup, and all your finger ends would be bleeding. And all these great big sheets to pull over them, we had to wash them in enormous sinks, and two of us had to twist them to get all the water out and syrup. After a year I'd had enough. My Dad was reading the press one night and said, "There's a nice little job for you here…at the Maypole in High Ousegate". We did as we were told in those days so I went there, I was 16.

Alan Benson started his apprenticeship at Terry's, at the age of 14 in 1939.

My uncle was the Engineering Workshop Foreman. That's how I got the job. Uncle George expected me to go into the engineering workshops. But when the time came, I went into the electrical department until I was 18 and I joined the navy.

In your apprenticeship you had to do six months in the engineering workshops. I was on night shift because we were making parts for Rolls Royce engines. We made a thing called a banjo, something to do with a carburettor and it was all aluminium work. They used us then as munition workers. You were given little jobs in case of air raids. And at the end of the workshops were about 15 cycle sheds. And they built some little air raid shelters with site slots in the brickwork, immediately opposite the big double sliding doors of Hill's workshop.

On the night of the Baedeker Raid, I was on Scarcroft Road then and we had an engineer who lived in Scott Street. Although the raid was fairly close, we were in the roadway watching all the fireworks, until a plane came across and fired a few bullets so we dashed in the shelter. I got on my bike when we finished next morning, to ride back to Scarcroft Road, and I went through Nunthorpe Grove. And it was just like a ploughed field. There was just masses of soil. I couldn't believe it was so close to where we were. I went to bed after lunch, and woke up at night to go on duty and Mum said, "You must have been tired. An unexploded bomb in Scott Street went off while you were in bed, and the roof's full of holes".

At Hill's, lorry-loads of this very thin wood came. They put all these thin layers together and cut them into manageable sizes. There was a veneer of wood, a layer of glue, a veneer of wood, and a sheet of glue. And they went to the press house, they had great big holes for the base part to be down at the bottom. It would press it at terrific pressure. And I was in there one night and one of the watchmen had been on his round and he was just sat having a rest. And the press exploded. I don't know whether the wood or the glue had got too hot. I can remember seeing this watchman falling backwards, the blast blew him over. These things were put on trolleys and taken to the workshop at the far side of the factory where they were cut into the right widths and lengths to make propellers. And then there was other machinery that turned the end of the propeller into a boss. They'd occasionally get crashed propellers sent in. If we finished our work on the lathes and we got our quota done, and we could get hold of one of these wooden bosses, we would turn biscuit barrels out of them.

At Clementhorpe, one of the things they made was strawberry chocolate. There was always a lot of waste and they'd send boxfuls down to Clementhorpe, throw them into the melangeurs, mix them all up and use them. And I ended up going to the dentist to have three teeth out in about six months from eating these.

Tank at Hill's during Second World War
(Courtesy Mike Grimes)

Irene McGouran

left in 1942 because there was a sugar shortage, and you either had to go fuse filling at Rowntree's or join the forces, so I was a WAAF, and I was in till '46. I came back to Terry's to the old factory down the riverside, and they were doing Chivers Jam. We were putting the lids on. And then when it came to strawberry time we were doing strawberries, taking the stalks out, it was a lovely smell. But you got your fingers burnt on the jars when you were putting tops on.

Irene McGouran 2005
(Courtesy Mike Race)

Mary Wilson née Robinson recalls how her grandfather Francis (Frank) and Uncle William (Bill) Lowther both worked as machine fitters at Terry's for 50 years. Frank retired in 1941. He had started as a boy of 12 in the lozenge department in 1889.

My grandfather lived in a Terry's house at 208 Bishopthorpe Road. He was a very kind man, one of the old school, very dignified. He had four children, Mabel, Bill, Hilda and Mary. Every Monday evening he walked from Bishopthorpe Road, going past barrage balloons in Hagyard's Field in Stockton Lane, to my mother's (Hilda's) house in Galtres Road, Stockton Lane, where she lived with her husband Ernest Robinson and my sister Margaret and I. He would come for tea and then he would play solo whist with my mother and father, and Biffa Barnacle, a very well known policeman who was a huge man in both size and spirit. I would be in the Morrison shelter which almost filled the room, trying to sleep. Frank always wore a wing collar and bowler hat. We had some good Christmases at the Lowther home on Bishopthorpe Road. I remember Uncle Bill was a wizard with clocks. He had a cabinet filled with little clocks, they were all going. It was his hobby. We were fascinated as children. There was nothing that he couldn't do with clocks and watches. He was a confirmed bachelor and proud of it, having grown up with three sisters, and he had a permanent stool in a corner of the Winning Post. When Frank died in 1953, Bill stayed in the house. Frank's daughter Auntie Mary was the last to die there. Although she didn't work at the factory, she was allowed to stay there.

The Lowthers were freemen of York. Henry Lowther, a coachbuilder, became a freeman in 1868, then Frank in 1898, and his son Bill in 1944. In 1996 my mother and I were able to become freemen through my grandfather.

Frank Lowther

(Courtesy Brian and Mary Wilson)

William Lowther 1940s

(Courtesy Brian and Mary Wilson)

Terry's Lozenge Department c1900. Frank Lowther is 12 year old boy.

(Courtesy Borthwick Institute)

In 1940, an event occurred at Terry's which had nothing to do with the war. The newspapers called it *'The Edinburgh Poison Case'*. In May, the firm received a letter from the Chief Constable in Edinburgh concerning some chocolates which had been poisoned. They were sent to Terry's to be analysed and identified by 'a chocolate expert', and it was found that four chocolates which had been originally from a box of Devon Assortment, two of pineapple, one dessert cherry and one truffle and marzipan, had each had their base removed by a sharp knife and potash crystals put in the cavity. They were then sealed with a paste of cocoa and water. The chocolates had been sent in a small crème de menthe tin to an 83 year old lady, Georgina Ferguson in Aberdeenshire, with an accompanying letter from a Brigadier General Tredegar, who claimed to be a good friend of her late son. It said that the chocolates were very select and had been a great favourite of her son, and that they contained grapes from French vines with crystals in them. The writer went on to say that 'doctors say they are rich in vitamins and health-giving'. The box was brought in to the lady by her maid and she tasted one chocolate but found it 'hot and unpleasant' and spat it out. As she had never heard of Tredegar, she alerted the police. One of the chocolates had the Terry's imprint on it and the York factory was asked for a list of shops in Scotland who had bought Devon Assortment between 1938 and 1940. Through visiting the shops, the police traced a boarding house proprietor, John Millar, and found a witness who had discovered some debris in the bin with a Terry's label and a carton labelled permanganate of potash. A handwriting expert was shown Millar's writing, finding it to be identical to that of the letter from Tredegar. A chemist from Terry's appeared in court to explain the technical side, and confirmed that Terry's never used dried crystallised grapes in their chocolates. It turned out that Mrs Ferguson's brother, named Agnew, had lived at the boarding house for 12 years and Millar had taken care of him, acting virtually as a 'male nurse'. When Millar had decided to buy a new establishment, Agnew had given him £6,000. On Agnew's death, Millar was the sole beneficiary of the £11,000 estate. The family were shocked by this and Mrs Ferguson had sought legal advice and was challenging the will. Millar had already bought the new guesthouse and was afraid he would not get the money so he had tried to poison the lady. Although he denied the charge of attempted murder, the jury at the High Court in Perth found him guilty and he was given 'three years penal servitude'.

Noel Terry got the MBE during the war for his work as Controller of Number 9 Group, Royal Observer Corps, in York. His son Peter served with the West Yorkshire regiment in India, the same regiment with which Noel had served in the First World War. Noel Terry recalls his work with the Observer Corps,

> next door to the Mansion House, going towards the river. York was the only city which had two observer offices, number 9 and number 10. Our main job was to trace on a map, and report to headquarters, all the movement of aircraft, our own and the enemies. I remember tracing a British aircraft which was over the North Sea, visible from the coast, and then it vanished. I'm afraid it went into the sea.

> I can remember the thing that struck me most was moonlight. You had a city blacked out and when you had a strong full moon, the way it lit up York was amazing. I went down on the night of the Baedeker Raid by bicycle. I had a stiff leg, I had one long pedal and one short. The worst was over by the time I got there. I saw some of the results. I remember in Blossom Street, on the road, bits of brick and glass. And I'm afraid I saw the Guildhall on fire.

But another member of the family was not to return. Kenneth, the son of Noel and his wife Kathleen, became a squadron leader with the RAF in 547 Squadron and received the DFC in 1942 but he died on 26th April 1944 at the age of just 23.

Stanley Parker writing in the Yorkshire Gazette in 1944, describes a visit to Goddards, when he was shown around by Noel Terry. He mentions the lodge where the garage and chauffeur's quarters were situated and describes going through the Tudor style arch, passing the marble cupid which 'raised its hands in silence'. Inside the house, he remarks on the long gallery of pictures and wonderful objets d'art including a rhinoceros horn. He is charmed by the collection of clocks, including the famous one handed clock. But then he talks of 'treading on hallowed ground' when he comes upon the framed picture of Noel's son Kenneth Terry, and notes the sadness in the eyes of Noel and his wife. Just as in the First World War, the Second was to result in many losses of people from all ranks.

CHAPTER FIVE

THE POST WAR PERIOD

Although the war ended in 1945, it took time for life to settle down again. There was a surplus stock of Air Raid Precautions equipment to be disposed of, and packs of gas ointment which had to be destroyed. 24 red danger lamps, 64 axes with belts and pouches, 24 whistles and 30 hand lamps were given to the fire brigade. Rationing continued until the early 1950s and certain items were very difficult to obtain. Terry's farm, the market gardens and allotments were still essential for use in the restaurant. Terry's had a Pig Club from 1948 to 1956 and they rented pigsties at Middlethorpe Manor Gardens for £1 a week. But they had to pay for bottles of pig drench, pig powders, pig remedy, pig meal, Epsom salts, sawdust, saltpetre and bars of salt. Malton Bacon Factory were very useful in taking the meat.

Terry's Fire brigade c 1958. Ernest Clayton on far left, Robin Terry far right.
(Courtesy Jacqueline Ake)

The plantation in Venezuela had survived drought and problems in the oil industry which made labour hard to get, but finally currency restrictions compelled the company to sell it. The board of directors at Terry's now consisted of Sir Francis, Noel and Peter Terry, George Stembridge, Ernest Clayton, J Robins (Robin) Terry who was Francis's son, Brigadier General C A L Graham and Air Marshall Sir John Baldwin, the husband of Noel's sister Kathleen. Francis had developed the manufacturing side over the years, and Noel the sales and administrative side of the business. It was Noel who designed the company vans to be mobile display units, as permanent exhibitions of Terry's products.

Peter Terry joined the firm after serving in the Second World War. He had been to Marlborough and then Cambridge before returning to York, where he spent most of his working life in the family firm. He was a member of the York Civic Trust and the Merchant Adventurer's Company, and was well-known for his sporting prowess, being described as 'arguably the best ever York sporting all-rounder'. Cricket was really his favourite game. He played for York Cricket Club at Wigginton Road, Yorkshire Gentlemen at Escrick Park (he hit his first century when still at school) and also in the York Evening League. One of his outstanding memories was of going to Berlin in the 1930s and playing cricket in a Germany v Great Britain civil servants' match in the Olympic Stadium.

He was also a golfer, and played squash and hockey for Yorkshire. He was a keen tennis player and at one time president of the York and District Mixed Doubles Tennis League. He gave the Terry Trophy for junior players and the company sponsored the All Gold Family Tournament when it began in York in the 1970s.

Peter explains his involvement,

> I joined the firm just after the war although I had worked there during the vacations. I was always on the sales side like my father. As part of my training, I went through all the departments then worked on the retail side in Liverpool. I'm afraid I had to sell Cadbury's chocolates and Rowntree's as well, although I tried to sell Terry's when I could. I also worked for a wholesaler as a representative. I didn't tell them who I was, I was disguised as Mr Peters.

He also recalls his first meeting with his Swedish-born wife Carin Scholander in 1948 at the home of Oliver Sheldon, a director of Rowntrees.

I knew him very well and he and his wife had the sweetest girl staying with them, and they didn't know what to do with her. They invited me to play bridge with them and that's when I first met my wife. I owe that to Mr and Mrs Sheldon.

Four months later they were married in Sweden. Another year later their eldest son, Anthony, was born, and was to be followed by six other children, Julian born in 1951, Louise in 1952, Robert in 1955, Charles in 1957, James in 1968 and Michael in 1970. Anthony recalls,

My grandfather lived on Tadcaster Road at Goddards and my parents lived in The Horseshoe for my first two years and then moved to The Beeches, a very nice Georgian house next door to Goddards. We were living at the bottom of his drive effectively so we'd often go and play in the garden. When I was six we moved to the Chantry at Bishopthorpe. It was very convenient for my father and he would very often bicycle in to Terry's from there. It was a Church Commissioner's house, we rented it for two seven year leases, then he bought a house in Brandsby in about 1969. We were always aware of the family business, always chocolates sprinkled around in the house. My grandfather was chairman most of the time I knew him, he didn't retire until he was 80 and he died when he was 90. We became known as the family who had lots of sweets around. In those days it was relatively easy to go in [to the factory], and not the health and safety precautions that came later. We'd go once or twice a year and take friends along. Occasionally there would be school parties arranged from my prep school in Scarborough.

Robin Terry had joined the firm in 1937, then served in the Royal Artillery from 1940 to 1945. In the post-war years, the factory went through a lot of reorganisation. The firm concentrated on the re-equipment and re-arrangement of existing machinery. The new trademark logo of a palm tree was registered in 1948. The main products were the assortments, the Chocolate Orange, the block chocolate – Bitter, Devon Milk, Oliver Twist – as well as Neopolitans, chocolate peppermint creams, boiled sugars, fruit pastilles and sugared almonds. A new type of pallet was conceived, made from metal, with the sides open, forming a cage. The workers could step inside to fill them and this saved space, avoided spillages and discouraged pilfering. They were stacked four high so that the height of the ground floor buffer store (15 feet) was fully utilised. The cages or pallets were moved by fork lift trucks and this was a speedy process. In the same store, the finished chocolates were run under an electronic metal detector. If any metal was detected, a loud bell would ring and the conveyor belt would stop. The product was sent to the laboratory to find the metal. Unfortunately, the metal detector was often triggered by workers with keys, money or metal objects on them, so a wooden rail had to be built between the worker and the machine to prevent this. Packages then went into a dark room to be x-rayed and finally pallets were taken by a Lamson elevator to the road or rail containers.

Mechanisation steadily came in over the coming years. The chocolate mill was in the single storey factory, where a giant duct provided air conditioning with an ambient temperature of 65 degrees Fahrenheit. Above the production line were two electric travelling cranes on the same track. Manual handling was reduced to a minimum. The cranes had a maximum load of one and a half tons. The cocoa bean store and cleaning department were separate from the mill, which helped with pest control. Beans were taken to the mill on Bev 1 ton electric trucks. Sample beans were assessed in small test roasters, so the blend was decided before the rest of the beans were roasted. The moulding room had rotary tempering machines on elevated platforms which were supplied with liquid chocolate through the pipes from storage tanks. Each mould contained 28 ounces of chocolate. The moulded chocolate went into cooling tunnels, before being transferred to the foiling and wrapping room, now automated, though some specialities like Terry's Bitter were still wrapped by hand.

Processes at the multi storey factory started at the top and cascaded downwards. On the fourth floor there was the manufacture of nougat, almond paste, toffee centres and sugared almonds, all the preparation of fruit and nuts for fillings. Fondant was made and various ingredients boiled, though this process had come a long way from the boiling department at Clementhorpe in the 1890s. Wooden trays filled with starch powder were conveyed under a board with wooden replicas and these were pressed into the powder and filled with ingredients before going down to the third floor with its enrobers, starch room and fancy moulding. At each enrober were four girls impressing distinctive decorations on the chocolates. The second floor was used for hand covering and piping. The first floor was the scene of packing and checking. The bundle foiling machines could wrap 90 chocolates a minute. The boxes slid down chutes to the ground floor with the buffer store, x ray examination and dispatch.

Terry's products were sent by road and rail to depots throughout the country and exported abroad. Special protection was given to chocolate destined for the tropics by packing in hermetically sealed tins.

The main laboratory was situated in the office block, and used for quality control and the examination of raw materials.

Nancy Fairbotham started at Clementhorpe in October 1945.

> I worked under Mr Brennan, sorting nuts and fruit. You had big trays and used to tip the nuts in and search through and take out any imperfections. And all of a sudden there'd be a beetle climb out. After a few months we moved to the packing room. All the girls I know today started at Clementhorpe and must have gone up in stages to Bishopthorpe. We were what you would call skivvies, we ran round after the packers, the older women, fetched and carried. There wasn't four conveyors then, there were still alleyways, women at the back sat like you sit at a computer today.
>
> In 1945, the men were coming back out of the RAF, that had been pilot officers, and there was one who had been **somebody** during the war, and they'd come back to pulling bogies around, and they objected to it. There were some arrogant ones amongst them. Fair comment, they'd had four or five years as officers, they'd done the lot. I got married in September 1953, and worked until I had children. You had to work until you were six months, you still had to lift and carry everything. They wouldn't do it today. There were two ends to the packing room, and the foilers and machines in the middle. We were at Mr Donaldson's end.
>
> When we started it was still Hill's ammunitions at Bishopthorpe Road, where the gardens are now. There was still propellers propped up, and aeroplane parts.

Of course the war had interrupted the normal work at Terry's, and parts of the packing room had been closed down.

> We were clearing Mr Hayhoe's end of all the 1939 stuff. They'd left all the silk casket boxes, the bows, the chocolates, everything, stacked in little alcoves at the side. In 1945 we ate the liqueur barrel biscuit chocolates that had been packed in 1939. And all the bows, you couldn't get ribbon in them days because everything was rationed, and they were breaking up these great silk caskets, and putting them in their pinnies. And they just threw the caskets away. There was one that was a bit like a barrel and it had obviously been hand done. I remember having a liqueur, and when you're 14 you think you've been drinking! The girl used to wear silk gloves to pack them, every chocolate she touched she had to wear these gloves. You had a camel haired brush to polish them so the top of the chocolate was silky. We had a boss Len Smith and we were terrified of him. He'd say, "There's a penny on the floor

down there". And we were all looking for this penny and it was one chocolate, we'd have to pick it up and dust it.

We used to make our own fun. I was threatened with the sack every week for larking about. I was always a joker. We'd put those brown layers of paper between chocolate, we used to wrap them round us, we did daft things. You could eat but if you were caught eating too much, you might get suspended. You would have got the sack for pinching, definitely. Every now and again they had a purge and searched you. We were innocent but you were scared, and if they told you not to, you didn't. You couldn't wear lipstick, you couldn't have earrings. Mrs Telfer came and if she thought your lips were pink she'd rub it off. You couldn't wear nail polish. There wasn't much around anyway.

I remember we'd ride down Albemarle Road and the carriage shop lads would be riding back that way and I can think of two couples who married after waving at each other on their bikes. Riding and waving and somebody would arrange a date.

Then I went to work at the bakehouse under Peter Gee. I can remember the men bread making, it fascinated you. They had a big slicer and it would slice a piece of dough off, and that piece was exactly the right weight every time. Just after the war you couldn't get fancy cakes, and Peter Gee would make all these fancies, and send them to Terry's shop. My friend worked there, and all the girls had to line up every morning like they were in the army before they were allowed to go in the shop and serve. All the dresses and the seams on their stockings were inspected. They'd have to have their hair a certain way. Oh poshness itself. They had a café upstairs, with silver teapots and everything.

When you got married, you bought a lunch for the girls you worked with. We would bag them up in little bags and buy a special cake and a couple of sandwiches. And you'd set all your presents out on top of the conveyors. I've still got the dinner service that the girls bought me.

Noel and Nancy Fairbotham's wedding in 1950s. Cake made by Peter Gee at Terry's

(Courtesy Nancy Fairbotham)

Terry's girls c1950. Back L to R
– Audrey Rafferty, Betty Greaves,
Elsie Howard, Doreen Forth.
Front – Minnie Ferguson,
Betty Sunley

(Courtesy Mabel Nicholson)

Nancy's friend Mabel Nicholson worked with her. She recalls,

At half past eleven it was 'Worker's Playtime', we knew every song there ever was! When I started I was so quiet. When I used to serve the packers, I'd call every one of them 'lady'. I was so shy. But they were all really good to me. I loved every minute of it. And the women worked the hardest, the men had it easy, they really did. I used to say, "If we come to work and don't do anything, we won't get any wages but they go to work and do nothing and get their wages at the end of the week!" The best job in packing was the All Gold, which was top of the range. And I got to pack them before I left to get married. I'd get to work for half past seven. My dad used to get my bike out for me and say, "I've put your bike facing Terry's". I'd bike to Terry's and I'd come home for lunch to Holgate Road, go back again and then work until half past seven. Any overtime, I did it.

Terry's group at Mabel Nicholson's
wedding 1950s. Front row –
Dolly Corrigan, Elsie Howard,
Mabel Nicholson nee Blackburn,
Doreen ?

(Courtesy Mabel Nicholson)

Dorothy Cowan, whose father had been chauffeur to Sir Francis Terry, went to work for the firm herself in the early 1950s.

Joan Terry [Sir Francis's daughter] got married to Chedwith Morgan Gwynne, he worked at Clementhorpe. He was something to do with the Ministry of Food in the war. He was a grand fella, and he got me this job but they made us redundant because Chivers parted company with Terry's in 1954. I was in the Sales Order office. It was small, about 24 of us. It was above the jam room. Ooh the lovely smells, marmalade and raspberry jam, and iced cakes. If there was a wedding or anything, Mr Gee would call us down, and show us the cakes he was doing and we'd get hot scones in the morning for lunch break. Drop offs they must have been, but they were lovely. I was a typist, I had a billing machine like a typewriter keyboard, they were all capitals, so it was faster. We did all the invoices. The orders came in batches and they were sorted out between the typists so we'd get certain areas. I had more or less the West Riding. A lot of them were catering orders, because there was canned peas and things, it wasn't just jam. They also used to freeze for Bird's Eye. Mr Gwynne had a little office at the back. He was full of fun, he'd make us work but we could play as well and we could have a joke. As soon as he heard that Noel or Frank Terry were coming, he'd give us the word and we'd settle down like mice.

The factory at Clementhorpe was a big old place, I once got stuck in the lift there and I'm petrified of going in lifts even now. Our office was above and one day I walked in and it conked out. And it was awful, because it was an industrial lift, no lighting, no nothing.

One of the factory drivers would bring waste to me dad at home, a pound every week, peppermint creams. I remember the restaurant, mum and I would go for coffee sometimes. They had dances in there. Cussons and Lights once had a dance and I think the Press ball was in there. They had a lovely ballroom.

Peter Binns began working for York Radio Relay at the age of 14 in 1947.

It was a wire broadcasting system and the idea was that you had one big radio station, you put wires and speakers in a house and you'd get radio. We used to do factories, Terry's being one of them. Because it was a big factory, it would probably drain all the power from our main amplifiers. At Terry's we installed a big amplifier, 500 watts, it was the old valve and mercury vapour rectifiers. They glow blue. They were fed from Parliament Street in those days with a GPO line into this amplifier.

The main thing was 'Music while you work', a half hour of music in the morning and afternoon. It was something they looked forward to. If there was some big national event, like the Grand National or the Ebor race, the union guys would say, "We want it on otherwise we're stopping work".

They had microphones, one in the gatehouse and the manager's office, if they needed to page anybody. One of my jobs was to keep it running. I'd go and clean the amplifier and check the valves and the voltage currents on these rectifiers. And if a department moved around, they'd want the speakers altering so they could hear the music. In the enrobing room, the chocolates go in these trays and the enrober pours chocolate on top. Then it would rattle along a conveyor belt to shake the air bubbles out. And it's a terrible thing to try and get over that noise. But you'd go in another room where they were doing the hand work, putting little whirls on the tops of chocolates, and it was fairly quiet. So it was a case of going in and putting up new loudspeakers, altering the volume because it was too loud for some folks and not loud enough for others.

The big amplifier was in the generator room. You'd get faults on speakers and one of the worse things was icing sugar. It gets sticky and that would stop the cone in the loudspeakers moving. If you went into the starch room where they do impressions for the sweets, they'd give you a white coat to wear and a visitor's hat. And the girls saw you and you got wolf whistles, and, "What's your name? Come round here. Are you taking me out tonight?"

One of the foremen used to say, "Bring your toolbox and leave it down there and there'll be something in it for you". And when you got back, there'd be a pound of sweets or slabs of toffee. I used to enjoy going there.

Max Drucquer started working at Terry's in 1953.

It was just before the Coronation. I got a job in the cost office and within a few years I was responsible for setting piece rates and making bonus schemes for the work force. Later on I worked with consultants who came into the company and improved productivity. Then I was invited into the personnel department. When I started, rationing had just ended, chocolate rationing being one of the last to go. At that time Francis Terry was still turning up at work from time to time. I remember him stopping me in the corridor once to say hello. He had travelled Europe to visit other chocolatiers, to bring in new skills. He'd go and see these things, come back, roll his sleeves up and do it himself. It was he who built it up to what it was. His son Robin was thought of as a successor. I knew him quite well. He became the works director but he was killed in a motor accident. I worked with Ron Collier six or eight years. He was quite a character. He'd been making jam for Chivers at Clementhorpe. Then he went into the personnel department. He was fun to work with. There was someone who'd been in the horse guards, and he'd spend his time standing to attention, Bill Hayhoe. It truly was one great big happy family. I don't think you'll get many people saying they hated it at Terry's. Everyone was approachable. Very few people stood on their dignity.

They built up a team of people which included me, to go about work study in a much more structured way, to improve productivity and reduce costs. In personnel someone had to do the interviewing of applicants for jobs, that was a large part of it. I had to look at the skills of different jobs and try to grade them. I got more involved in recruiting office staff and management staff as well as factory staff. You were still a name to conjure with, people in York worked at Rowntree's, Terry's or the railway. If you had a relation there, you would moreorless get a job.

We made Curiously Strong Mints, which was a question of mixing a paste with sugar and peppermint and starch and stirring it all together. And conversation lozenges were exactly the same, different colours like violet and rose, and words like 'Kiss me Quick'. Beautiful sugared almonds they made, I can hear the noise now of them tumbling in their copper pans. The chocolate mill was 100% men, everything else was 90% women. Some of the processes were very primitive. Chocolate Neapolitans in a shoebox, done by hand. The speed with which they wrapped the box and tied it up in string was something to behold. The welfare officer, Kath Brazier, or Mrs Telfer as she became, was a sympathetic person. One of her jobs was to visit the sick and take things round to them. If a relation died, she'd help them get probate. If anyone died in the company there was always a member of management attended the funeral. We employed women from Askham Grange prison, a section where the prisoners can go and live in small houses in their last year and take up employment. A woman from the Labour Exchange used to see Ron Collier and latterly me. We refused to have people who'd done bag snatching or shop lifters. It was very hush hush. But it was part of Terry's duty, to help people. The most we had at any one time was about eight. They were treated exactly the same as everyone else. And they had a bit of a nest egg to go home with.

It was paternalistic. There were five members of the Terry family there when I was there. They had a good pension scheme, and wages were controlled by the Confectioner's Alliance, with two or three unions and big companies who got together and negotiated basic rates of pay. I've never gone along with the myth of the idle British workman. Most people in employment work hard. Course you get ones that don't, but by and large, at Terry's and Rowntree's, people took pride in their work. They wanted to make good chocolate. People didn't get sacked from Terry's, it was remote.

After the war, the Castle Museum opened a Terry's shop.

The man who did the work designing the shop was Alf Davis. He insisted on sugar mice being made specially for it. He told me that white mice have pink tails and pink mice have white tails. He went in 48 hours before it opened to the public in about 1948, and said, "This is fine but there's something missing. It doesn't smell right". He got the chief chemist, Walter Turner, to come up with something in a bottle, they had it for years under the counter and the smell pervaded.

In 1950 Noel Terry announced that the firm's exports totalled £12 million, compared to £2 million in 1939. In the 1930s, girls over 18 earned 29 shillings a week compared to 69 shillings in 1950, with an incentive bonus, and labourers had earned 53s which doubled by the '50s. The new National Health Service meant that workers would receive sick pay and holiday pay from the state. There were now canteen facilities, and an excellent lunch could be bought for 1s 2d.

Joan Pannett returned to Terry's after the war and found big changes.

At the beginning of the war they told us we had to go into the forces. They were altering the factory. I went to work at the aircraft factory. When I went back after the war, I couldn't believe how it had changed. You could sing and talk for half an hour on a morning. And we had some fun, though it was really hard work. And when Christmas or Easter came, we worked from seven o'clock in a morning until six at night. Sometimes seven if they had a big order in. You felt as if you lived there. We had more money which was good but it was never ending. And Saturday till three o'clock. So all you had off was Sunday.

The overlookers were always all right with me. If you did your work, they were very nice. When I went back, Lol Cussons was our foreman. And the girl who sat beside me was Violet Elmer. Her son played rugby for York. And Lol was rugby mad and he'd come over to see her on a Monday morning. And she'd say anything to him. I thought, "What a difference between Len Smith and the managers now".

But Violet was a character. We'd be sat foiling eggs [at Easter] and we were on this belt with them coming down, and she'd say, "Are you all sitting comfortably? Then I'll begin". And she'd start telling a story. At Christmas she got dressed up as a fairy, and she'd run along all the belts in a dress of organdie, and a big stick with a star on. She'd go up in the lift and round all the other parts and they didn't say anything to her. She was a born comedian.

Before the war, you wouldn't have dared to be seen putting a sweet in your mouth. You would have been suspended. When I went back, Violet was a real chocaholic. As they came down the belt, she just took one off, she'd be sat eating lumps of chocolate. That's how relaxed it was.

The tradition of whole families working at Terry's continued. Eileen Carter's father Thomas Frederick Carter, known as Fred, was born in 1906.

He left school at 14 and worked at Lipton's then went to Terry's for 50 years, making jam for Chivers during the war then in the pastille department. His brother Thomas Henry, known as Harry, was a foreman there, he did 50 years too. The other brother Ernest worked there. They were related to Harold Milner, cousins I think. My mother was a hand coverer on piece work [working in the enrober room decorating individual chocolates]. Rowntree's were always very keen on the hand coverers from Terry's, because they were so good, so well-trained. Then my sister and I worked in Terry's offices. You started off in the Registry, then I went into Powers, which was the forerunner of computers. We had to punch cards. Our boss was Mr Gossop and Barbara Garrett was in charge of Registry, and trained everyone. My sister in law Margaret Scott also worked there, in comptometers. Dad played bowls for Terry's and did a bit of gardening for them at Vine Street. I played hockey, and we wore the All Gold shirts, brown skirts and gold socks.

Eileen later went into teaching and became deputy head at Archbishop Holgate's school.

Terry's Cricket Team c1930. Fred Carter is on left at front, Francis Terry in centre
(Courtesy Eileen Carter)

Terry Ellis was an electrician with the company. He started work as an apprentice in 1956.

My father, who was the manager of the restaurant and café, pulled a few strings for me. I got a call from him, "Can you get to the main office and ask for Mr Clayton?" So I'm on my bike pedalling down to Terry's. "I'm Terry Ellis to see Mr Clayton". I waited and waited. "Come in". I stood there shivering. "Yes?" "I had a message to come and see you about a vacancy for being an electrician". "Who told you that?" "My dad told me". "What have you brought with you? Any reports?" "No". "You'd better go and get some, hadn't you? On your bike again, my lad". So again I'm pedalling up Poppy Road, sweating, raked out these reports, same procedure, up to the office, knocked on the door, waited. "Come in". Showed him them. The report said, "More interested in the girls than doing work". He said, "A man after my own heart. You've got the job". But he was a terror. If he saw you walking, slumped over, hands in your pockets, he'd shout from the top floor window, "Who do you think you are? Get your hands out of your pockets".

I did day release and one night class. Sometimes we went down to Clementhorpe but 90 per cent of my time was at the Bishopthorpe factory. We started off on days, then got put onto shifts. You were there for insurance purposes, if the mill or the melangeur broke down. But as years went by and the new plants came in, they had to work them to the limit, so they started the twilight shift for ladies who had children, from half past five. We also had the maintenance of the front shop. There was only two sprung dance floors in York, Terry's and the Albany. And at Terry's after the functions, they'd go up to the Oak Room, and we'd roll the old carpet up to make room for the dance floor.

In the old engineers' shop, at the top end was the welders and the big forge. We'd have a tie on, which was frowned on later on, because of health and safety, but if you had this posh tie on, George Collins would come with a big pair of scissors and whoosh, off with the tie end and he'd hang them up. And we were encouraged to make certain tools. Percy Barnett was the foreman, "Take it up to the welders and get it forged". George would say, "I can't do it. Ask your mam to send you with some maiden's water and I'll do it for you". We were putting in a new conveyor in the cake wrapping. "Terry, go up to the stores and ask him for the shortening tool". So I went. "It's up on the top floor, so-and-so's got it". Then I went up there and, "We've sent it down", so I'd go down, "It's broke, you can't have it". But it was all good humour.

We'd decorate the factory at Christmas, each room with streamers and they'd bring cakes and sandwiches. In the canteen, they'd have the staff performing, they'd sing carols and Peter Mortimer would play trumpet. It was Christmas dinner and nobody would go back to work then. We had the annual works dance in the canteen. It was embarrassing at times with all these women. In the cutting room, where they'd put toffee on big blocks, splash it all with flour, they was like snowmen, the girls. And you had to get under [the benches] 'cos the switches got all starched up. And this girl, I was underneath the machine and a foot come right between my groin, "Terry, how long are you going to be?"

Terry's wife Moira worked at the factory. If they were slack in one department, the women would be moved around. She recalls,

I was in the enrober. And then the packing room, but I've worked everywhere. I didn't like the starch room. You had to wear Wellington boots. We used to sing, you'd do different things to occupy yourself, 'cos of the boredom. Once he [Terry]

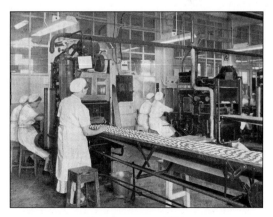

Enrober room 1952
(Courtesy Mike Grimes)

came in with a ladder. We'd sing, "James, James hold the ladder steady", and he went bright red. You used to put your knees under t'belt to stop it, so you could have a rest. We all used to. But they was good hearted there. I mean the times we had at Christmas. We'd do eggs and they'd bring rum, brandy, whisky, wine, and drink out of half the egg. [Terry's mother] was as mad as a hatter. She used to get wigs on and everything, when we'd go on nights out.

Terry recalls that they had known each other since childhood.

We lived down James Street. We'd go out gangs of us, to the baths and pictures altogether. When she was in the enrober, I used to go up, and, "What are you doing tonight?"

The things we did! The management knew though. On the roof we had fan houses. We grew tomatoes and would swap them with the lasses for a few sweets. And then down in the bean warehouse, where the girls used to make propellers [in the war], there was a big cellar. It was really humid, and we'd grow mushrooms in there.

In the chocolate mill there was a big machine with rollers. Frank Douglas was a chocolatier. He made sure the chocolate went into the depositor, and that chocolate had to be a certain temperature to stop it going white or to make mouldy chocolate. It was in a big tank, like a vat, going round and round, steam heated with cold water. It had to be exactly the right temperature. They didn't have a thermometer or anything, he knew the trade, just by dipping his finger in and putting it on his lip.

David Meek recalls his time as an apprentice electrician,

To be honest there was never anything nasty done to you. Of course they'd send you to the stores for a 'long stand', or for elbow grease, or buckets of steam or a skyhook. You thought you were men of the world but you all fell for it. It was a super place to work. The men were real nice fellas and they sort of carried you along. We thought a man of 40 was a granddad, when we were 15. There were crowds of men and they'd have given their right arm for you. At Christmas, in our little department, the men always bought the apprentices a Christmas present. In those days, it was something.

We did all the installation. If they built a new department or a new extension to the factory, the electrician would do the electrical work, the joiners would do the joinery work and so on. And similar with the fitters, but some rooms would have a dedicated fitter, especially where there was wrapping machines, 'cos they're a very technical thing. But we had a roving commission. We got used to the girls, they were the salt of the earth. They once tried to make some wine out of blackcurrant pulp at Clementhorpe. They had it under t'bench but it gives off a vapour, and my uncle, chief electrician, came in one day and he could smell this stuff. "By the way, when I've gone, get Frank Hargreaves", [the plumber], "These drains need rodding". And he knew what it was! Basil Hall, he used to have the dirtiest, filthiest mug. We called it 'pyorrhoea mug'. And one day somebody washed it and he nearly died. "It's lost all the flavour now".

They had a big building department there, joiners, plumbers and painters, it was self contained, nothing ever went outside. For the first six months as apprentices, say if a man was over 40, you called him Mr. Then they would say, "Right from now on, David, you call us Harold", or whatever. I'd be about 17, it was winter and our foreman came in and he had this electric iron. Under supervision I repaired it and he said, "It belongs to Sir Francis Terry. You better take it up", to Middlethorpe Hall. And it was snowing like high heaven. I went on my bike, knocked at the door, and the butler came. "Lady Terry wants to see you". And she said, "That's for you, thank you very much for mending the iron". It was a pound note. The snow was so deep and I had to push my bike, and coming up the drive there was this big car, and it pulled up and it was Sir Francis. He always wore those astrakhan collars on his coat. "Who are you?" I said, "David Meek, sir. I've mended the iron, sir". "I had a Henry Meek, was he your father?" "No sir, my grandfather". Then out with his wallet, a pound note, "Happy Christmas". I said, "Oh no thank you sir. Lady Terry's just given me a pound". "Yes, and I'm giving you a pound". So I got two pound. And I always remember, 'cos my wage at that time was one pound six and a penny.

Audrey Foster, now Lambert, worked at the restaurant for two years and then moved over to the factory.

I worked on a conveyor belt, where the chocolates came down, and we'd to sort them. I liked all the company, all the girls. You had your breaks and your lunch and you all went to the canteen and time passes. And we'd go out together on a night.

Although most people agreed that the women worked harder than the men, at this time there was no sense of resentment. Audrey says,

That was the way it was. You'd often see the men stood talking.

But it was the meeting place of Audrey and Tony Lambert and the scene of a number of romances.

Tony was going out with one of the other girls. She was nice as well! I used to ask her where they'd been at the weekend and she'd say, "We didn't go anywhere, he went fishing".

Then Tony and Pam fell out and I'd fallen out with the boy I was going out with, and we just got together. We'd meet up and sit and have our dinner together. Then he just said, "Would you like to go to the pictures?" He'd send me notes down on the conveyor belt. And people would bring them to me, all on Terry's wrappers, All Gold. I've still got them. Nearly everyone starts, "I'm sorry…" 'cos he'd either gone fishing or forgotten he was meeting me. But it was more romantic then, it was nicer.

And then we used to go up on the roof somewhere and sit with our sandwiches, holding hands. It was a happy time, a fun time, because when you're young, you enjoy everything. Tony would meet me on a morning and we'd cycle to work, and then he'd cycle back home with me.

Tony and Audrey Lambert's Wedding
(Courtesy Tony and Audrey Lambert)

When we got married, we had some beautiful presents, they were all over the table up in the dining block. And lots of the girls came to the wedding. There was a piece in the paper about it, 'Mother gives daughter away'. It was quite unusual then.

Tony worked in the Almond Paste department, making centres other than creams (which were made in the starch room), various types of toffees with nuts in, and fudges.

It was on the top floor, and Mr Carter was the boss, and I'd go and fetch things from the stores like coffee beans. There was a gang of four or five on machines and I kept them going.

We did all the centres, and they'd go on to a big machine and get cut into different shapes, diamonds and squares, and then go somewhere else and get covered in chocolate. At the other end, they would boil the toffee. They put it on a big cool table and cut it up, it all got printed out into individual toffees.

There was one big room of all the centres. The girls would have a little pan with hot water in, and they'd keep the soft liquid warm. They'd throw a cherry in, whip it round and put it on a tray, and that would be a cherry centre. And there was a rum truffle paste in there. The rum was very strong, we'd try it now and again. Neville was in charge and he'd say, "Get a bit if you want", but you only had it once, it was a bit strong, more like an essence.

Then ginger, that would all be in barrels. It was like treacley syrup, and a bit further over was the pineapple, in rings in big tins. You'd put them in like a pastry cutter and put a lid on, and push it down and they'd cut into segments. The Almond Paste room was mostly men, with just one or two girls dipping these cherries. I did National Service, came out in 1958 then went back into the packing, then into transport. I had a pair of wheels, I'd put all these chocolates on, get a metal hook and pull 'em along the floor and leave 'em at the side of the machine for these girls. The girls lifted them off. I'd have maybe fourteen or fifteen trays of chocolates. And they'd go for waste or mis-shapes or packing. But I was keeping three conveyor belts going, with four or five girls on each.

We worked in our jeans and shirt, there were no overalls when I was there. But a lad called Wacker Ward had a brown coat on, he was an overseer. He'd chase you about a bit and keep you on your toes, and half the time he was talking to the women. But you knew your boss and you kept out of his way and you did your job and nobody ever bothered you. As long as the girls didn't run out of chocolates.

You could get searched. There was a big, tall man stood under the archway. If he caught anybody, he'd been tipped off. The sweets were quite cheap to buy, Terry's waste, and sugared almonds, which was really nice.

Where the enrober was, everybody had hats and masks on, there was all sugary dust flying about [starch]. A machine would make an imprint in the tray of flour and then a bit further on there'd be some liquid squirted into that, and that would be a centre for a chocolate.

I played football for Terry's with a lot of other lads every Saturday. We'd go down to Vine Street, and a real nice man took us for training, he always said I would be some good at football, they called him Freddie. It was floodlit and we had training down there with showers. We trained on a Tuesday and Thursday night. The pitch was going out towards Bishopthorpe. We played in amber and black squares and black shorts, with amber and black socks. I think we were in the third division in York and District.

And I was a very keen fisherman. We had two internationals, Harry and Fred Duncanson, absolutely top notch anglers. I'd go down to Terry's Avenue on a night and watch them fish. They'd make their own floats and were two very nice men but very competitive. The club had six matches a year. You'd go to the River Nidd, the Ure, the Derwent and down to Boston.

We had a trophy for CATSA, the Confectioners' Allied Trades Association. They had matches all over the country, with two or three hundred people fishing. Terry's had five teams. We had a bus and we'd go down. In 1958 I fished for the A team and we won best team, and I got a trophy for that. And two years later we went down to the Boston Forty Foot, and I won the CATSA on my own. I got presented with the angling winner in 1962. The trophy was presented by Robin Terry. He came to the City Arms and we had a good night.

Terry's had a nice recreation hall, two snooker tables and a table tennis table, I'd go in there on lunch breaks and have a knockabout. You'd gulp your dinner down and try to get on first. There was a chap called Geoff Pears, a van driver, and he married a girl there and they won a lot of table tennis for Terry's.

Table tennis team, late 1940s.
Front row – Lol Cussons, N Hudson, Peter Terry
(Courtesy Borthwick Institute)

Betty Hartas, who started work in 1944, moved to the Personnel Department in 1955.

We were responsible for everything to do with the wages, had to work out the increases, and we had a set of rate codes starting at 001. And 006 was a female on full rate. Our department was responsible for keeping files up to date, and for new starters, we had to make up a record card. On Fridays, the company doctor came at 11 o'clock and they used the welfare office to examine patients. Anyone who had been off sick for a month had to see the doctor. We had to keep records of all sicknesses so that we could write to them and tell them that an appointment was being made. And holiday pay, that was quite a big task. If they were leaving, we had to calculate how much holiday pay. We had to pick out the staff who'd done 25 years so that they could be invited to the meal at the front shop. We were responsible for the cycle racks. And there were about ten sheds with racks all numbered. We had a chart with these on. And when you think of how many cyclists there were at Terry's, it was an amazing thing to keep that in order.

They did a company profit share scheme. But to qualify for this, you had to be there from the 1st of January to the 1st of January. And I started on the 3rd so I didn't qualify the first year. Then the third year we got three and a half week's wages. I think we all nearly went abroad on it. It was wonderful. But it was finished the following year.

Jean Winship started work in Terry's offices at the age of 16 in 1953.

When you started you worked in the post room and did all the errands, taking files around. After three or four months you were moved on, and I was with Mr Tebbitt in planning and production. They had an office full of people typing, they got moved on to be secretaries after so long. Peter Terry was there and Robin Terry, they walked round. They were lovely. We had our break in a morning, we'd go to the canteen. You didn't have coffee and tea in your office, it wasn't heard of. I was in a little room with another girl. And our boss Mr Nesbitt was in the next room and there was just a partition between us. When he wanted us he'd knock on the wall! When he was sat behind the desk, if the phone went and it was one of the Terrys, he'd jump up and stand to attention.

We'd cycle to work, and there was one day and it was quite icy. Four of us would cycle to work together, and we'd turned into Knavesmire Road, and a bread van was coming down far too fast, and when he came to turn the corner he skidded, and knocked all four of us off our bikes. Fortunately we were all okay, just a bit battered and bruised, bikes a bit dinted. We had to push our bikes, and we had to go in to see Mr Gossop. Petrol was on ration, so they had to decide whether they could afford to send us down to the police station in a car to report it! Anyway they took us, but fortunately this chappie in the bread van had reported it as well. But Peter Terry gave me a lift a time or two. If we were setting off to walk and he happened to be passing, he would pull up and give you a lift to Tadcaster Road. He wasn't toffee nosed or anything.

Jean left after four years and went back to an evening shift when her children were small. She found quite a difference between the office and factory.

That was an eye opener! You even sat in a separate canteen, cut off from the office staff. But for all it was manual work it wasn't as hard. You didn't have to use your brain, it was physical work but not mentally exhausting. Some of the girls when they were talking, it opened my ears, I was bit naïve. I'd had three kids, but the things they used to say! But they were lovely, and they were all married women trying to get a bit of extra money for your kiddies. That was the only time they could come out. I did Easter eggs where you wrapped 'em in foil, and I cut ginger. You all had your own knife, and woe betide anybody who got your knife!

It would come whole, and you had to cut it into shapes that they could crystallise. You'd to cut the edges off and waste as little as you could. You did it all by hand on a marble top. You'd weigh it and you got paid piece work on how much you'd cut. And I did oranges. When I first went they'd do it by hand and the Chocolate Orange would fill these little moulds. Two of us were in the hot end pushing them through. Then they went into a cooler and were banged out into moulds. They'd clamp them together and a girl would pipe the core to hold it all together. But eventually it was done by machines.

Terry's hockey team 1955. Jean Winship second from left on front row.
(Courtesy Jean and Brian Winship)

They encouraged sport. When York City got to the semi final, in 1954, they had it on the tannoy. People couldn't go so they broadcast it.

I played hockey for Terry's. We'd train at Vine Street, they had a nice pavilion. But we'd play on Knavesmire usually. And we'd play netball. [Terry's Ladies Netball Club was formed in March 1957. They received a grant from Central Sports Committee and could enter teams in Allied Confectionery Association League to play in different towns].

They used to do a swim from Clementhorpe factory up the river, it was a mile. And that was every year until health and safety stepped in and told them it wasn't safe to be in the river!

Girls football team 1930s
(Courtesy Borthwick Institute)

You'd sometimes row in boats, because they had to have so many go up with them, near the swimmers. The girl who usually won was Moira Winspear, her dad was a security chappie, and he was really tall so they'd call him 'Tiny Winspear'. One of the nurses, they used to call 'Dearie Darling', because when you went in it was always 'Dearie' or 'Darling'. If you were not feeling very well and you went to the medical they gave you a drink of ginger, because that 'cured everything'. And if you were off sick, the nurse came round once a week and brought you a jar of aspic jelly. [Calves' foot jelly]. Terry's were a family firm and they really did look after you. They were lovely to work for.

Then Jean met Brian Winship, an apprentice machinist. Many couples met through the social side of the company, at dances, through sport or seaside trips.

Brian would organise dinners for their department. When I won the Miss Maytime in 1957, it was a social night for the Pastille Department and all the women and girls went in for it. They had so many picking out girls and we were just dancing and I won it. There were three prizes, and one was a perm, and I'd never had one in my life. And they put all these curlers in, I thought my neck was going to break! But we had some really nice outings. Benny Lister, Tony Lister's brother, that had Clifton Ballroom, was over that department, he would organise social nights.

Jean and Brian Winship on left
(Courtesy Jean and Brian Winship)

Brian started as a messenger before taking up wood machining.

Everybody wore crêpe soled shoes then, and I went up to the fourth floor, and in the middle they had the boiling pans. This chap called me over, "You better go now, son, you've been here long enough, the boss has got his eye on you". And I couldn't get away. The floor was that sticky, and with crêpe soled shoes on, the soles left the shoes! But we had a way of sticking 'em back on, because we'd go round to Pastilles, and there was Gum Arabic in them, so if you chewed a couple of pastilles, got all the sugar out of them, stuck 'em on your soles, they'd stick your soles back together.

I had the full training, and night school at Ashfield. We did everything the factory required in wood – door windows, springs, trays, morris boards, pallets. We had a fully equipped joiners' shop. In the building department alone there were 86. There were four joiners permanently up at the main factory, nine in the joiners' shop on assembly and three wood machinists. I was at Vine Street, all the vans were serviced and stabled up there.

There was never a lot of overtime but if there was, tradesmen always seemed to get it. But it wasn't to do with production. [Every August] they shut down for the factory fortnight, and we had a certain amount of work to do. You got periods when you were slack, but days when you had to keep your nose to the grindstone. You had to keep the joiners going all the time with materials. You clocked in at half past seven, and by twenty five to eight all the machines were running. They had parquet flooring, and it had to be maintained. We had to sand them, and seal them while the factory was shut. And if you'd got your jobs done, and the painters would be behind, you'd go and help them out, like wash the ceilings for them.

Everybody mucked in, we all helped each other out. It was the only fortnight that you got into the factory to do jobs, and there was always more work than people. Plumbers would probably have sixty panes of glass to put in, and you'd chip the glass out for them. We'd go up to Noel Terry's house. I worked there for about six weeks re-facing his greenhouse, with a plumber.

Chivers was at Clementhorpe when I first started but the building department changed it back over for Terry's. There used to be an underground tunnel, vaults underneath, they'd produce jam at one side, send it off to the other side, using pipes, jar it all and then it'd go in this underground conveyor to the five storey. They left about 1955. The printing department came back, the little white mints came back. Sugared almonds came back, and pastilles started up in a big way when sugar came off ration. All five storeys, [at Clementhorpe] except for the second floor, was taken up with pastilles.

The ingredients were sugar, gum, gelatine, glucose, citric acid and flavourings, mixed in jacketed steam pans. A machine could mould eight to ten boards a minute, each of which contained 200-300 pastilles. These had to set before being coated with a crystalline layer of sugar to preserve them, and then they were packed into two ounce tubes and four ounce boxes. The manufacture was eventually transferred to Bishopthorpe Road.

People had been starved of confectionery. You got what they called a monthly fancy order. You were allowed maybe a couple of Chocolate Oranges, and half a dozen bars. You got your Easter eggs, what you wanted for your kids. And you got so much waste a month. There was a fair bit of pinching went on, there were a few caught and finished when we were there.

Clementhorpe got flooded regular. We were on flood patrol at least twice a year. They'd say, "River's expected to come up so much tonight", so we'd go down there and all the big roller shutter doors at the front, we used to put 'em down and bolt 'em in position and then fill them with clay, so the water couldn't get in, it would come up the drains! Front end always got flooded. The boiler was built fairly well up so they could keep the factory going. It was lower at Vine Street because it was on flat land.

Clementhorpe was nearly all Terry's, and on Bishopthorpe Road, they owned from the car park right up to the Archbishop's Palace. We converted [Middlethorpe Manor] when Frankie Terry died, into three flats and when Lady Terry died, they sold it. There were loads of cottages down there that butlers and chauffeurs used to live in.

There was a motto, which was – 'Rowntree's have Dunollie [Convalescent home at Scarborough], but Terry's had Clementhorpe'. Cos it was easy at Clementhorpe, you had no management. When they decided to close Clementhorpe down and put it all under one umbrella, to save on boilers, blokes would literally nearly start roaring, [crying] because they had to go back to Bishopthorpe Road. Clementhorpe and Vine Street were really good days.

There were two people that kept Terry's in line, one was Len Smith. He'd come round Tuesday and Friday, and everybody was on their toes. And the other one was Mrs Telfer. "Your nails are too long, what are you doing with lipstick on?" Things like that, they really was keen. But they kept that place together, the backbone of Terry's. We had the ten percent men. They'd come with tools, selling you kitchen buckets, or sinks. You could always get off 'em whatever you wanted, you always got a wheeler and dealer, in those places.

I was a joiner until I had a car crash in '68, and put my shoulder out, and I wasn't able to carry on with me job. You had to carry eleven by fours and things like that, to saw them up and make joists.

When I came back to work, I went to the chocolate mill and I'd tank chocolate to the departments. There was the five storey and the one storey, but in between there was nothing, and when it rained you had to stop loading. So they put a covered way in. The storage tanks for Bindler 5, [the German machine] were on the ground floor. We'd fill these half tonne tanks, pull two at a time on an electric truck up to the third and fourth floors, pipe it into the big 20 tonne tanks they had up there. Then

I got promoted to a team leader, and I would sample all the chocolate, check the viscosity, make sure the thickness was right, find what department wanted what.

The starch room was a bad room, it was fairly up to date with modern moulds, but it was a dusty department, that was the trouble.

We would make conveyors, and they started off on a spindle, And I suggested we put two halves in, extend the thing out. I got paid for that. And at the mill, when the refiners used to start up, they'd throw chocolate out at you, and quite a bit of waste went on the floor. I suggested they put a metal arm, where the rollers was. It used to throw chocolate up and these arms used to go over and stop it. I got well paid for that actually. It was a good suggestion scheme.

We always had leaving parties. The Winning Post used to do really well out of us, and the Slip at Clementhorpe. Terry's was built round it. The kid that had it, his son was a driver for Terry's. The kid that had St Clement's Club at that time, he used to be in the starch room at Terry's. So you knew everybody.

The Terry's Waifa Bar came out in the 1950s, and became a competitor to the Rowntree's Kitkat, though on a smaller scale, but it became very popular. Terry Ellis recalls,

The baking plant was massive. It would play up at times. We had to short the mains out to light the main gases.

David Meek was also involved,

They said, "We're having trouble with the Waifa plant. If it won't start, short out 7A and 7B", but he actually meant 8A and 8B. So we went in there, shorted these two out, and I'm not kidding you, the biggest bang you ever heard, all these doors flew off and bye, some muck came out. The little fella that ran the department, Icky, he stood there and he was covered in soot and he says, "Well we better put kettle on". In that department, there was a young chap and he was an artist and he used to do these funny pencil drawings. And he did a drawing of this oven, and I'm stuck.

The drawing showed David scratching his head, saying, "Well brother, we've done it this time".

Some of the workers were asked to be factory guides and Joan Pannett became one in 1950.

If they got two or three parties coming round at once, they would call the older ones out. You had had some knowledge of it. You started in the cocoa beans, went into the sugar boiling, the enrober room. It was interesting because I'd never been round the factory before. I remember I took Robin Terry's son round, it was his birthday. Six of them came and if they weren't sick before they got home, I don't know who would be. They were eating chocolates one after the other.

They bought a machine from Germany and it was going to do away with packers. It had hands to pick sweets up. Well you've never seen such a carry on, they got us all round to watch it. There was chocolates going everywhere, up in the air and onto the floor. And it had cost them I don't know how much, 'cos they'd had to move the belt out of the way. It wouldn't go at all, it was picking the wrong sweets up and squashing them. It just had to go back.

Factory guides 1950. Back – unknown, unknown, unknown, Len Smith, Irene Martindale, Joan Clark. Front – Sybil ?, Kath Moyser, unknown, unknown, Eva ?

(Courtesy Joan Pannett née Clark)

Another important royal visit took place in 1957 when Queen Elizabeth II came to York. Rowntree's, Terry's and Craven's together presented her with an elaborate gift. The casket was from Asprey's of Bond Street, and cost £38.6s.8d. It had three drawers and self opening doors in green niger leather, elaborately gold tooled with special motifs symbolising the cocoa bean. The Arms of York were made up of inlaid leathers and gold tooled. The drawer knobs were in silver gilt, engraved, with a total cost of £115. The contents were a selection of confectionery from all three companies.

Peter Terry recalls,

> We concentrated on the quality side. Our prices were higher than other people's but I hope the products were worth it. Our motto was 'Terry's for quality'. We had a marvellous chemist who was always working on new products and new innovations. He brought a box of these new chocolates to Sir Francis and thought, "He'll like these. This is something unique". And Sir Francis tasted one and they were thrown out of the window. So they had very high standards.

Sir Francis died in May 1960 and his obituary described him as a 'big loss to York'. He was a leading figure in the civic, industrial and political life of the city, and High Sheriff of Yorkshire from 1945-46. He entered the city council for the Guildhall ward in 1924, and was elevated to the Aldermanic bench, made a magistrate and received his knighthood in 1936. He was Deputy Chairman of Yorkshire Insurance and chairman of York County Savings Bank, and later president on the death of the Earl of Harewood. He had a long connection with York Conservative Association, and was president of York County Hospital. He was a generous patron of York Cricket Club, patron of York Harriers and Athletic Club, and Clifton Cycling Club. He took an active part in the welfare of these sporting organisations, with a keen interest in education and was a generous benefactor to St Peter's School, helping to make the new wing and extensions possible. He was interested in agriculture and very keen on riding and was vice president of Yorkshire Agricultural Society.

Noel took the place of Sir Francis as Chairman of the board, Peter Terry succeeded George Stembridge as Sales Director and Harold Milner, son of Thomas, the works manager and a director, also became a director. He had joined Terry's in 1926 and served in the war.

By the 1950s, Bill Godfrey, the Terry's representative, was working much further afield.

> I was covering Northern Ireland, a big area, for five and a half years. Ireland wasn't so prosperous as the mainland and this affected our sales. It was a bit of a battle. They had a big shipyard strike at the time when I was there.

Things gradually improved. We changed policy and some of our lines were rather compact in the packaging. We were running tubes of fruit pastilles, the same price as Rowntree's, threepence. I could sell everything they could make so I was given the whole production. I could go on a Saturday morning and visit three or four wholesalers and get a thousand items. We were doing so well that the managers decided to put them up to threepence halfpenny, and my pastilles went zum [down]. The chief Rowntree's representative went on a training course to America and I could see the way things were going, so I started to study for my Institute of Marketing, I studied for a couple of years and passed. The firm were informed but it didn't make any difference. I was living at Jordanstown, a lovely district of Belfast.

Fuller's manufactured in Ireland. So they were very strong, especially on the border areas. The Catholic community, some of them were extremely friendly. But you could feel it with certain districts [mistrust of the English]. They came round but they didn't give you a free hand.

It was most peculiar because you got in a village, two shops, the Protestant shop and the Catholic shop. Neither of them were really doing enough business to keep going, and they both treated you mainly as, "Oh you're English". Of course I observed all the niceties. I raised my hat to the fathers [priests], and so on.

It varied so much in each area. If you go to Hull and you go off to Newcastle, you would think you were in different countries, as far as the trade was concerned. Some of our outers opened up with a bit of display stuff, simple little cards that went into the window, that said Terry's. But no advertising, generally it was just word of mouth, Terry's was accepted by all as quality. But when we came back to the bread and butter stuff, it was tough. We did extremely well with Easter eggs, and Christmas stuff, we had a whole range of fancy boxes. And we could never get round a complete journey before we started to sell out. Then suddenly one day, they said, "Will you go to London?"

We had an office at Marble Arch, a beautiful place. The showroom was all walnut showcases. It was on the second floor and there was a little place to park, which was a big thing. I did the west end, Knightsbridge, Harrod's, I never saw any country. Parking meters had only just started and that was a terrible thing. When you called on Selfridges you had to queue to see the buyer. He bought at certain times and there was usually a queue. And then you tore out of the shop and round the corner to a little snack bar and you tore into there. From the sublime to the ridiculous. The

Queen used to have bitter chocolate and she had to have it specially delivered. So I had to get an order down to Harrod's. We had £3 boxes of chocolates with ribbons and some of them were bought by the hundred. It was fantastic, the biggest turnover in the business. But it was a drive, I would have killed myself if I'd gone on there 'cos the tempo was so hot. You'd go into one of these big stores and the buyer would give you about 15 minutes and you were still trying to sell them as they were walking away.

We could sell more than we could produce. And in London it depended so much on the weather. A nice hot Saturday and Sunday and everybody went away. If it was a miserable weekend, you rubbed your hands.

I was in London for four years. There were people like me working to death, and extra business to be got, and out in the sticks there were chaps twiddling their thumbs for little orders. Where I lived down to Knightsbridge took me nearly two hours. So not only a hectic working life but hectic travelling in London. I'd spend every Thursday in Soho and at night, go to the theatres.

If you went to the upper circle you saw 'Terry's' on the tray. Then somebody from Terry's went to London, went to the Lyric Theatre and reported to the manager that there were no 'Terry's' on the tray. I said, "You should have gone into the circle, the dearer seats. You'd have seen it then".

CHAPTER SIX

THE CATERING

Restaurant 1920s
(Courtesy Mike Grimes)

Terry Ellis was an electrician at Terry's and his father Norman was manager at the restaurant, and also in charge of the outside catering. Norman's brother Jack was the chef.

My dad started as a pageboy. Then he went in the kitchens. The front shop sold sweets, cakes and bread, which was made at the factory in the bakehouse. There was also the restaurant and the café upstairs. And there was the outside catering which was separate, run from the office. Everything was done by my dad and his secretary. When he'd go about a job, they expected him to get tapes out and measure everything, but he'd just look at it and, "Right you'll want a certain size of marquee, so many guests you'll want so many vol-au-vents, so many pounds of smoked salmon", and Jack would write it down in his little notebook. They had some marvellous functions. Every week there was something, especially when the

FANCY BOX
No. 5757
Packed with
Two Pounds
DEVON
ASSORTMENT
10/– each

FANCY BOX
No. 5755
Packed with
Two Pounds
DEVON
ASSORTMENT
10/– each

CALVES JELLY
Packed in
1/3 and 2/6 Vases
also
Pint and Quart
Bottles

CHOCOLATE BURNT ALMONDS

[Terry's] Packets

5/– Net One Pound Pkt.
2/6 ,, Half ,, ,,
1/3 ,, Qtr. ,, ,,

CHOCOLATE BRAZIL NUTS

[Terry's] Packets

5/– Net One Pound Pkt.
2/6 ,, Half ,, ,,
1/3 ,, Qtr. ,, ,,

CHOCOLATE GINGER

[Terry's] Packets

5/– Net One Pound Pkt.
2/6 ,, Half ,, ,,
1/3 ,, Qtr. ,, ,,

LANGUES DE CHAT
2/- and 1/- Boxes

CROQUETTES
9d. each

NEAPOLITANS
9d. and 4d. Packets

HUNTING CHOCOLATE
Five Flavours
1/- Boxes

TABLETS
3d. each

PASTILLES
(DROPS)
Oval Boxes
6d. each

PASTILLES
(DROPS)
Round Boxes
2/- and 1/- each

BITTER CHOCOLATE

CAKES 8 oz. 2/- each
4 oz. 1/- ,,
2 oz. 6d. ,,

DESSERT
CHOCOLATE APPLE
2/- each

SPARTAN
BARREL
2/- each

DESSERT CHOCOLATE
ORANGE
2/- each

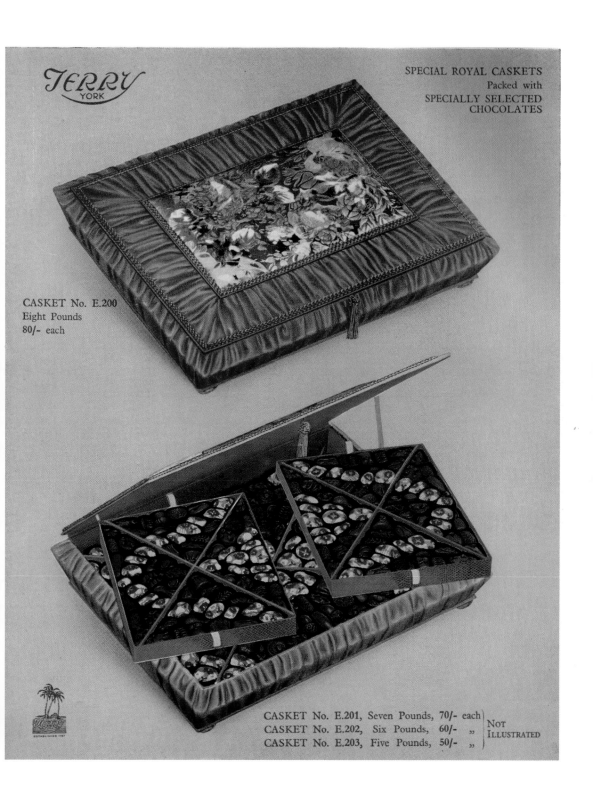

Terry
YORK

CASKET No. E.200
Eight Pounds
80/- each

CASKET No. E.201, Seven Pounds, 70/- each
CASKET No. E.202, Six Pounds, 60/- „
CASKET No. E.203, Five Pounds, 50/- „
} NOT ILLUSTRATED

1½lb MOONLIGHT (STAIRWAY) 05821   3 per outer

1lb MOONLIGHT (PIANO) 05784   6 per outer

-116-

show season come in. Coming out balls, weddings, agricultural shows. My dad liked everything to be on time. If he rang, "I want a marquee up in Dunnington", that marquee was up the day before.

Front shop 1930s
(Courtesy Mike Grimes)

Front shop window 1921
(Courtesy Mike Grimes)

Everything was put into big white containers, put onto a lorry, tables, chairs, covers, silverware, plates. The calor gas stoves were packed into this wagon. Everybody had their own little job. Barker, Lee and Smith in Beverley, they was cattle food producers, and they'd invite the community of farmers into their marquee for sandwiches, tea, coffee, cake, vol-au-vents, and sweets – fruit salads and sherry trifles. My mam would do all the cutting up. I'd say, "What you cutting them up for? It's a farmer's hand, they want half a sandwich in their mouth". There was about six in a pile, then gone. My mam was manageress, over the waitresses. They used to deal with Boggs of Bridlington. And there was always a policeman in St Helen's Square and we'd been to Boggs one afternoon, come back late in the evening with this box of lobsters, live. They called the copper Sandy, "Well Norman, what you got in there?" He opened the box and these lobsters were [poking their claws out]. But I thought it was cruel. I once read that you've no need to put them in boiling water. They used to scream like mad. He had a big galvanised washtub and he'd put it in the kitchen 'cos he'd get mainly fish supplies from them, fresh.

Oldfield's supplied the main champagne and wines, the fruit came from Young's in Micklegate. Otherwise all the bakery stuff [came from Terry's], and Jack would cook all the meats. And sometimes at Riley Smith Hall [in Tadcaster], the chefs would go and cook the meals on the job. And he had the waitresses lined up and there wasn't a thing out of place. He'd walk in front, and march them up all in line and they'd branch off at each leg, and then as soon as the top table was served, everything was in, and if one thing was just out of place he'd twig it. It suited some of them just to work at the weekends at weddings or banquets.

Restaurant window 1925
(Courtesy Mike Grimes)

They'd ship them out in a coach. But they were tiring days, setting off from St Helen's Square at half past seven, not getting back till next morning, working right through the night if it was a banquet or a 21st or coming out balls. Then they had to pack everything back, lift them all in, washed and cleaned. And if there was even a teaspoon missing, there was hell on. We even did the main jointing, the joists and the pyro work. When I was in a marquee, I put the chandeliers up, all the way down

Front shop and stairs to restaurant 1930s
(Courtesy Mike Grimes)

the middle, and the sockets for the band. And I'd go and fix up the supplies. And that's why I'd get dressed up. I'd do the announcing.

Before they went to Clapham's, the marquee people, they used to have their own. We'd get the canvas laid out, had to go up the guy ropes and put the flags on and the light fittings. We were at Market

Weighton one day, putting this tent up and it was windy. We'd have to pull the guy ropes up, and if you didn't get them on quick, whssh, away it went. Well this old bloke come up in a mucky old hat and wellies. "Would you lads like a drink?" So he brought these two crates of beer out. I says, "Oh good. What's the old codger like here, will he miss it?" He says, "I am the old codger!" Then later he come out in top and tails.

The main event we did was the Royal wedding, that'll never be forgotten. [The Duke of Kent to Katharine Worsley in 1961]. The girls from the factory were the waitresses. They used to draw them in when there was a big function.

There was a buffet for a thousand guests in a 30 foot marquee. Betty Hartas helped out.

It really was wonderful. It was a champagne reception but if anyone asked for whisky they could have it. This old waitress said, "There's a tray, don't let anybody have it 'cos you'll be useless without it". Then Terry came running over, "Somebody's giving Princess Margaret a whisky and they haven't a tray". I said, "I don't care". I hung on to my tray and Princess Margaret got her whisky without a tray.

We went by coach from York [to Hovingham], so we didn't see anything of the wedding here. But this marquee, it was the first time I'd ever seen one all draped in beautiful pastel shades. There were three huge wedding cakes. When it was over, we sat down to a meal, and we had exactly what they'd had.

David Meek also recalls,

Sometimes we'd go down to the front shop. If you asked them for something to eat, they'd give you it, Norman and Jack. But if they saw you pinching owt, they'd tan your backside. In those days, Terry's never had a licence, if you wanted a drink, you had to go round the corner to the Half Moon. Every day when you went in the shop at four o'clock, it was all gone, nothing left. And next day it would all come again. And the girls wore lovely maroon uniforms. Everything was spotlessly done.

Peter Gee, in the bakery, did all the icing. He was a genius. He started at Terry's as 'flavour lad', taking the flavours to all the departments. He had a basket with all bottles in. A little bottle of mint would flavour thousands of mint creams.

They used to kid Norman, used to say he was the worst paid man in Terry's, which he would be if he'd got an hourly rate. Cos he worked 27 hours a day some days.

I remember going with him to do the electricals, to Mrs Brotherton's at Kirkham Abbey. And she owned 'Freebooter' that won the National years ago. Norman said, "Are you lads interested in racehorses? I've arranged for Mrs Brotherton to show you [the horses]", and she took us off. So he had some nice ways about him.

Norman was brilliant. If you had 500 people for a dinner, he knew how many bread rolls you needed, and how many pork chops and all that. There was never any waste. He knew exactly how much.

Function at Terry's Oak Rooms 1970s. L to R – Bill Arundale, David Meek, Betty Hartas, Lol Cussons, Shelagh Flanagan, unknown.

(Courtesy Betty Hartas)

Audrey Lambert's first job was in Terry's restaurant in 1954.

It was waiting on the tables, and being taught silver service. You had to be able to talk to customers and had to say what you thought was nice for that day. You had to look smart, and be a good time keeper. It's hard work though. From the restaurant you had to go down these flights of stairs to get the food and then come up with it. I was young and nervous and Mr Ellis was very strict. There was a lot of older ladies when I worked there, only two of us that were young. Some of the ladies had worked there for years and years. We wore a black skirt, black top and white lace pinny.

At half past seven [in the morning] you'd everything to get ready, the tables to lay, the cloths to put on, and then you had everything to clear up at night. There's quite a bit to do before a restaurant actually opens. These ladies would come in for lunch, or at eleven o'clock for tea and scones, or for afternoon tea. There were proper lunches, they always started with soup, main course and a sweet after.

Mr Ellis would come in. You never knew where he was going to sit. He'd say, "What do you recommend for lunch today?" You had to say, "The beef's nice", or whatever. You had to make sure that everything was spot on. He always thanked you afterwards, and he'd leave you a nice tip.

I think it was 15 shillings a week, I remember giving me mum ten shilling and I had five. Out of that I had to pay bus fare, and get stockings, 'cos you had to wear black for work, and make up. There was just me mum and two sisters, and so she needed it.

It was beautiful stuff they had. It was quite expensive so they were those type of people that sit now in Betty's window. There were ladies who always sat at the same table, and they were quite miffed if they couldn't sit there, and they'd be there for an hour or two with coffee and a cake, chatting away, with their posh bags.

[I once spilt some soup] on a lady's suit. She put her arm up and I caught it and it ran right down the side of her, and it was a lovely suit she had on. I started to say, "I'm awfully sorry". And with that he was there behind me and he said to the lady that the suit would be cleaned, and it was just smoothed over like that.

Terry's restaurant 1928

(Courtesy Mike Race)

Cocktail bar at restaurant 1920s
(Courtesy Mike Grimes)

Brian Winship worked at the joiners' shop but would help with the outside catering,

> *in my spare time, nights, to get extra money for the kids. Sometimes you'd get three or four jobs in a week, they had permanent staff, but they never had enough, because some nights they'd have two or three on in one night, one at the front shop, one at the Merchant Taylor's Hall, one somewhere else. I used to run the bar and did a bit of waiting on. We did a big job for Birds Eye once, about 500 at the Assembly Rooms. I worked in the Mansion House when the Lord Mayor used to have his parties.*
>
> *They had mobile kitchens. They had a wagon and, everything was taken off and put in a marquee. The main marquee where the actual dinner was being served, but at the side they had a small marquee for the catering contingent.*

But then in 1965, tragedy struck. There was a function at Newburgh Priory, near Ripon and Norman Ellis was badly burned when a gas cylinder blew up in his face. He needed plastic surgery, and it was the end of his career. In February 1966, he was awarded £20,000 damages by Calorgas Ltd. Terry's were told they had no liability.

David Meek recalls,

> *He couldn't go in the front shop after that. They lost all their big catering jobs because they knew Mr Ellis and that he'd do a good job. The people who took over, I'm not decrying them but they hadn't the skills, 'cos he'd built them up from being a little boy. He knew everything but had nothing on paper, it was all in his head.*

In hospital his hands were wrapped in plastic bags, and eventually, he was like a snake, takes the skin off. It was an experimental thing they were doing with him. He went into work for something and they told him just to leave the premises, 'cos of how he looked. He got better as time went on, but that upset him, 'cos Terry's was his life and soul.

In the 1940s and 1950s, Terry's Ballroom was used by a number of organisations, such as the RAF Association who held their Grand Masked Ball in January 1948, with dancing to Norman Holmes and His Band. In March 1948, the RAOC had a Benevolent Fund ball at Terry's Ballroom, dancing from 9pm to 1am to Walter Garrard's Orchestra, tickets including supper were 10 shillings. Other well known local dance bands performed

Stairs and light in restaurant 1930s
(Courtesy Mike Grimes)

at Terry's own dances, as in January 1952, when music was offered by Jack Carr and his Melody Aces followed a few days later by Harold Midgeley's Orchestra.

Maurice Grimes was born in 1931 and came to York when he was 20. He had been a chef in Torquay and then in the army.

I started at Terry's as second chef. Meat was rationed, they only allocated you so much, say 40 lbs of lamb. There were only so many restaurants, Bettys, Terry's, the British Restaurant in Jubbergate. We used to make a lot of beef croquettes, chicken cutlets, fish cakes, omelettes, you had one meat a day either roast lamb or beef, but you could get liver and offal, and braised oxtail. And we sold tripe and onions, had a lot of regular people for that. We had rabbit, it wasn't rationed, and a lot of jugged hare. We'd get them from the game merchant. You had a game licence, they were the only ones who could sell it to you, Johnson and Elson. We sold a lot of ducks, 500 a fortnight, had to dress them ourselves, the kitchen porters would do that. We used to get through ten gallons of soup a day. And soup in a cup to take out. We

Terry's van
(Courtesy Mike Grimes)

had a big stockpot. It would take 60 carcases and lamb bones. We did all the outside catering as well in between our work, catering for 300 as well as cooking.

After a few years they opened the chef's room, we had a serve yourself place upstairs, a carvery, the first in York. It was around £1, no more, meat, veg and soup. That was 1963. So we sold meals downstairs and upstairs. The waitresses had to come down 42 stairs. Towards the end, there was double staff, two wash ups, two washing machines, they couldn't get round that one.

We were full most of the time. For a banquet, we'd have 290 for a sit down meal. Then the Oak Room above that would take about 30 for special occasions. We also catered for Yorkshire Insurance next door. They'd built a bridge across to the Oak Room. They had that every week for a director's meeting. Our own directors would come in every week.

The restaurant site stretched right back to the Judges Lodging in Lendal. When the circuit judges came to the city, they took up residence there.

When they had the Assizes, we'd send their breakfasts round to the lodgings, or to the Mansion House.

Many a time I've gone to work at half past seven in the morning, worked right through the night and come back at half past seven in the morning, and not have any sleep. We used to earn more in overtime sometimes than the wages. The best time was Yorkshire Show, but we started quarter to six in the morning to get to the showground before they closed off the traffic, had to get food and everything in.

We cracked 30 dozen eggs there for scrambled eggs. We had big white catering boxes and you pre-cooked most of it. You had to cook the chicken and ducks and if it was roast beef, all cut into 20 slices. An apprentice from Terry's put it in with damp greaseproof to keep it hot on the calor gas. Roast potatoes were done in the frying *pan, we used to pre-steam the potatoes, and somebody would roast them for half an hour, and fresh veg we used to cook there.*

We'd do a lot of work in the Assembly Rooms and once did 380 vegetarian lunches there. About ten of them were vegans and they sent a lot of their own stuff like dandelion milk. It was new then, they'd got television cameras and were filming in the kitchen but hadn't enough cable to go through. Our kitchen was all stainless steel, we'd get them [health inspectors] come round to check it. We had a little hand wash basin. They came round and said, "Congratulations, you've got some soap". I thought, 'There's no soap in there!' When he went, it was a potato that had been through the rumbler, [a machine which peels potatoes] it had gone pear shaped. Somebody had tipped some potato water in it and it looked like soap.

Things were seasonal. You only got cucumbers when they were available, now they're all mass produced. The freezer was mainly for chickens and ducks. As things improved, you could get frozen veg. You'd get 34 lb halibuts, fillet it all out, fried halibut was a favourite. You don't see many halibut now, or if you do, it's a small piece. The biggest we had was 41 lbs. We'd get four stone of plaice, put in egg and crumbs. We'd get about 500 lbs of salmon, not farmed salmon, proper salmon. Smoked salmon was 17/6d a pound. We had an accident once. They let us have a lot of pans for storage from the factory. We stuck this halibut in on a Friday, it was frozen, put it in to thaw. A chap doing the washing up, he put the lid on [he didn't see the fish] and more pans on top. The following Thursday you could smell something. And nobody had noticed, 'cos of the loads of pans.

Once at five o'clock at night, the waiter said, "There's 30 people come in for plaice and chips and they'd booked". We started crumbing all this fish. They were about to sit down and [someone from] Bettys come running across and said, "It's our customers". We had to put the fish in the fridge for next day. Sometimes if sausage rolls or vol au vents came back, we put them in the shop. We did all our own baking except Cornish pasties, they were bought in. We had a puff pastry machine. We had square tins for any mashed potato left over, and all the halibut picked off the bones, boiled up and into fish cakes, with parsley, for a shilling each. We had one old lass made fish cakes all day long. The frying oil that was nearly finished, we did fish cakes in that and it went into milk churns and to the soap factory. Two pounds a milk churn. That's the chef's perks, and so much for the swill. They had pigs up near Terry's. We had to sell our swill to him. He came back, "I've got something for you, 20 knives, a bit of a candelabra". That was the waitresses, they never noticed it.

We were famous for our Madras curry, got our picture in 'Country Living'. We had bolognaise and chicken kiev, common today but not then.

Every Burns Night we catered for St Andrew's Society. I went round the room with whisky and haggis and a piper, and would present the haggis to the Master and he used to bless it, and give us a drink of whisky.

Maurice Grimes at Terry's restaurant, Burns Night.

(Courtesy Mike Grimes)

We did the venison dinners for the Merchant Adventurers, very dry. We would cook it in a big pastry case, in a flour paste dough to keep the moisture in. Four haunches of venison we used for that feast. There was a dance most weeks in winter. They had a dance for the Glassworks staff and a load came from Rowntree's, one department.

At Well Hall near Bedale, we did a hunt ball, the officers used to come down from Catterick. They had a marquee and we rolled a carpet out. Then the lady asked, "Oh I say, are you going to sew it up?" About a thousand metres of carpet! Then, "It's a bit bare, can't you bring the furniture from the two rooms in the house, and the piano?" It was a grand piano and we broke the leg off and we stuck it back on again, she didn't know. And big armchairs and sofas, and a bookcase 20 feet long up to the ceiling. We kept them all in order but by six o'clock in the morning we were a bit tired! We did balls for the army, always had a firework display, a lot of jobs at Tadcaster for various lodges, and at one hunt ball, Mandy Rice Davies came and Christine Keeler and Profumo was there. They used to bring all the debutantes up from London by train, they would wear ball gowns. Somebody picked the lock on the swimming pool and they were throwing all the girls in, with the drinks in their hands. We lost loads of beer mugs in the bottom, were trying to get them out with a window pole. Someone, half drunk, gave me £5 for a bucket of ice water. We did all the shows from Peterborough up to Edinburgh.

Raby Castle, we did our last job there, she gave us £10 each. It was hard work. The kitchen was where coach and horses go and we had three flights of stairs to carry

*everything up. We did a wedding at a social club in Huddersfield, we used their
kitchen. The wedding was at half past two. Well in Huddersfield at 12 o'clock, the gas
went down to a little thin candle. We couldn't get to our calor gas, all the cars were
parked in front of our van. We delayed the wedding by an hour, the only wedding
we were late with. Peter Gee did all the wedding cakes. We had one with three tiers,
and a false bottom tier and they came out with an army sword and crunch, straight
into the wooden cake.*

*We did a lot at the Mansion House. But it was a long way up to the state room, and
it wasn't made for all this catering. We did two or three jobs a year there, we did the
Queen there twice, then the Duke of Kent came, and Peter Scott, the wildlife man.
Then when the new Mayor came, it was in the Assembly Rooms.*

*There were ten of us in the kitchen plus waitresses. When Fortes took over, [in 1963],
they sent us stuff from the M1 cafés, 3 cwt of mashed potato powder and a machine
to make chips. They had no idea. Loads of stuff we never used. Like Smash, and
you put in a big cylinder and cut up chips at the bottom. I remember one day we
were running late, we had the whizz kids from Forte. We had boxes piled up and,
"Where's that going, chef?" "A dinner for 300 people". "Oh how do you do that?"
Then one came round to see if we were wasting money. At the back of the kitchen
we had a room, with old crockery and hooks to hang hams up. Lady Terry sent us
a big York ham. They went and looked at this, old fashioned ham, four inches thick
with fat and they had me in the office, "What's this, ham with four inches of fat? We
can't buy things like this". I said, "It doesn't belong to us, it's Lady Terry's, it's private".
He shut up straight away.*

*If we wanted confectionery from Terry's, like chocolate vermicelli for the black forest
gateaux, we'd ring the factory and they'd come down in big five gallon drums. We
made all our own desserts. We sold loads of tinned ham in the shop, Terry's bought
it, forward buying, 200 cases of seven pound tins of ham. In them times you were
just starting to get melons. It was a rarity. We were starting to get things imported.
My black forest gateaux were a favourite, used to make 20 or 30, damson ones and
pineapple ones.*

*The Terrys had their own wine cellar, but kept it in St Helen's Square. The under
manager handled the wines, it was Ian Martin, father of James Martin, the TV chef.
When Forte came, they opened all this wine up and said it had to breathe and the
corks had been out an hour and a caterpillar had hatched out of the cork, must*

have been in it for years. They put a beachcomber's bar in the Half Moon in Blake Street, they had to have an exit, and it was into our kitchen, their fire door. They had to break the glass to come through. We weren't happy about that, we thought they'd break it when drunk and come through, but they never did.

Private functions at the restaurant had a choice of 12 menus. For the outside catering,

hors d'oeuvres ranged from smoked trout or salmon, pâté maison, turtle soup, cream of pheasant, prawn cocktail, crab bisque. Fish included Dover sole, turbot, poached salmon and grilled halibut. There were pastas, then meat included coq au vin, duck a l'orange, mixed grill, fillet steak, escalope of pork, roast leg of lamb. Vegetable in season, usually cauliflower, broccoli, sprouts, beans, peas and carrots. Sweets included peach flan and cream, lemon meringue pie, bread and butter pudding, blueberry cheesecake, black forest gateau. There was a Terry Pack take-away service for busy workers.

Banqueting menus had a choice of five plus three in winter.

For example –

Menu no. 1

Consommé mimosa
(garnished with tapioca, French beans, royal garnish, hardboiled egg)

Filets de sole Veronique
(glazed sole fillets served with grapes)

Chateaubriand grillé printiniere
(centre cut fillets grilled and garnished with asparagus points, artichoke bottoms and small champignons. Watercress and lemon)

Crème renversée and grand marnier
(crème caramel served with Swiss cherries flambé)

Menu no. 4

Tortue Claire
(clear turtle consommé soup served with cheese straws)

Bouchées de ris de veau
(blanced sweetbreads cooked with cream and served in vol au vent cases)

Pintade vigneron
(guinea fowl roasted with red wine, garnished with grapes and lemon)

Petit pots au chocolat
(delicate chocolate mousse in small pots, topped with chocolate cream)

The restaurant and catering business closed down in 1980. Maurice stayed there until the end.

> All the furniture and cutlery and everything was all sold off. £30,000 they got for it. They gave all the staff something of Terry's, shrink wrapped in plastic from the factory, like the Terry's teapot and cream jug.

Mike Grimes, Maurice's son, worked at Terry's in later years but recalls his father's work.

> These chef programmes they get, all bawling and shouting, there was none of that at Terry's. I used to go in the school holidays and wander into the kitchen, nobody questioned it. You didn't have a big turnover of staff either. People enjoyed the job, didn't want to go anywhere else.

> You could buy 12 different types of coffee, either ground or roasted beans. A man in the factory spent all his life roasting coffee beans. We'd make our own coffee liquor to flavour coffee fondants with. He had a set of scales and a range of different beans. It was unbelievable. After he retired, no more coffee.

It was only open in the evenings in later years.

> In the 1900th celebrations, 1971, Terry's was one of the first places that stayed open till ten o'clock and started the Celebration Restaurant, open from then on four nights a week. Going out to restaurants started to become more popular. Today you can go to 50 or 60 in York.

Terry's Ladies Table Tennis Team c1950
(Courtesy Borthwick Institute)

Terry's Swimming Gala - Rowntree's Baths c1960
(Courtesy Borthwick Institute)

CHAPTER SEVEN

THE 1960s

Charles Forte was born in 1908 in Mortale, a small village between Naples and Rome. His father Rocco moved over to Dundee, where he opened a small ice-cream shop. The young Charles was educated at boarding school in Rome, but left at the age of 17 determined to succeed in his father's line of business. He set up his first 'milk bar' in London in 1935. Soon he moved into catering and the hotel business. His company became Forte Holdings Ltd, bought the Café Royal in 1954 and opened the first motorway service station in 1959. Eventually the Forte Group expanded into a multi billion pound business, with Little Chef, Happy Eater, Crest, Travelodge and Posthouse Hotels as well as having a majority stake in the Savoy Hotel. His was one of the greatest business success stories in post-war Britain.

Throughout the 1950s and 1960s he continued to buy strings of companies. Most, like the Kardomah cafés, and Fuller's, were in the catering sector, but he also bought part of the publishers Sidgwick & Jackson and a stake in the Catholic Herald newspaper.

Peter Terry with Mr & Mrs Charles Forte
1967

(Courtesy Mike Grimes)

Profits had been low at Terry's between 1958 and 1962. Rumour of a takeover bid was mentioned in the Yorkshire Evening Press as early as January 1961. Serious talks began in February 1962 and in 1963 the Forte Group took over the company. Peter Terry explains,

> My father always thought we ought to be bigger. Forte was interested in us. He already had a lovely factory, Fuller's, near Hammersmith, which eventually became a hotel. He sold the site and brought Fuller's production up to our factory. Forte was very charming and used to come up to every other board meeting.

The Lord Mayor of York at the time, Mrs Mona Armitage, was quoted as saying that she didn't know whether Terry's had been 'fortified' or Fortes had been 'terrified'.

Bill Godfrey continued with the company,

> Forte offered to buy Terry's and they didn't have a lot of shares because they'd sold them all. But Noel was offered a directorship on Forte's board. So he agreed and we were taken over. Fuller's had done badly, sold stuff on sale or return, and that's fatal because they'll stock it and won't trouble to sell it. They took the Forte's people and put them in charge at Terry's, although the Terry family still had positions of authority.

> They offered me the job of General Sales Manager of Fuller's. And the only thing we had was a sales force, and the stuff was being made in Ireland. And I couldn't see it lasting. Fuller's mint lumps was their big line. They had a whole range of stuff, and their cakes as well of course.

> With Forte it was a different ball game. When I'd moved to London, the only help I got, was my goods and chattels carried down. When I moved back to York, after Forte's had taken over, I was given all sorts of aids, stuff for curtains, estate agent paid, this and that, which made a difference. They devised a bonus system and set targets, and I moved to York as Area Manager for Scotland down to Nottingham. I had 11 reps and two or three merchandisers. So that was exciting. I was responsible for their training, their work, their targets. If a chap wasn't meeting a target, I went and helped him sell.

> Forte's were _for_ advertising, the old Terry's regime were very much against it. First of all we advertised Moonlight with wholesalers. It really did its stuff, there was no doubt about it. So we went into advertising the Waifa Bar, and did very well

with that in Yorkshire because there were a lot of market traders. I'd say, "Give me sixpence an outer off and I'll guarantee you a sale to one person of 6,000 outers". I'd do a lot of promotions, and we were beating Rowntree's in Yorkshire.

In one advertisement, Terry's announced, 'Don't forget this is 'Be Sweet to your Secretary Week'. How about giving her a box of Contrast?'

The world is changing all the time. And some firms have that magic, you can't put your hand on it. Terry's were number three after Cadbury's and Rowntree's. But we tried to follow the big ones and that can be fatal. With a niche market, they'd still remain. We spent £2,000 on two ads for Chocolate Orange when it burst into the market on television. All sorts of people bought them, it was an absolute winner. But you can't maintain

Bill Godfrey and awards. 1960s
(Courtesy Bill Godfrey)

it. We got rid of our sales force, I was still selling through agents. Then they asked me if I would take the marketing over till they found somebody. We had two advertising agents and I did a lot of changes in the period. Changed the packaging, did a lot of research work. We were a small firm so I could go across to the factory and speak to people. It was very easy co-ordinating. When I ended up with 12 assistants, it was agony to get things done.

Forte paid out money for this idea and that idea, and they wanted things that suited them. Every Forte hotel gave you a Waifa bar with your tea. Forte gave away a lot of 1767 to his friends. He went to the Café De Paris and gave away his favourites.

Fuller's products did not last long as the factory did not have the space and time to promote them.

Sylvia Brough was born in York in 1934 and began working in the mint room at Terry's, then also did 'special packing' part of the time.

I started on the top floor with a man called Jimmy Wells. He'd make his paste and put it in this machine and press it down with a big wooden spoon. I had to use what we called Farina, like powder, so it didn't stick. I had gloves on, and put this stuff on trays to dry out. They'd be stamped as they came out of the machine, the little white mints. When we had nothing to do I'd go in Caramel Cutting. And there was one job that fascinated me, and it was cherry dipping. They had this hot fondant, and the cherries all had to be stoned and cleaned. They were sticky, and the ladies would pick them up and put them in the hot fondant. They had a tool and they'd dip them in. The trays had grease proof papers on so they didn't stick. They used to be so quick, it was marvellous. And then I worked in the cutting room, where they'd make brazil nut caramel, fudge and nougat in big pans. They were hand cut. The other sweets were moulded so they were always the same size. The packing machine would accept the moulded sweets, but because the caramel and the nougat weren't the same, it used to throw them all over the floor, it was so funny to see that!

You had to buy your overalls then, and turbans, and you had to get them white. We used to boil them. Then they got a laundry and it was nine pence a week to have our overalls washed. Then the nylon overalls came in, but I never liked them. And our turbans starched beautiful, I had two or three.

We had a special packer, Betty Spreadbury and she taught me to pack and I absolutely loved it. When they were doing the silk caskets, they'd ask me to help. We'd pack in little brown cups, not trays. We had sponges to wet the cups, no licking your fingers! Then you got these thimbles, and that was easier still.

Charles Forte wanted silk caskets for Irene his wife. He would have a big six pounder, it was beautiful. And we'd send them to Italy to his friends and family. There was about twenty we did for him every Christmas. They moved us to the far end of the building on the first floor. I always said we had the best view and the best job in the factory. And although he later sold out, we still did all his orders for him every year till the day I finished.

We used to have a show in London with all new samples and new boxes. One year Hazel Palmer and me went to London, on the train, they took us to the hotel. There was Cadburys, Rowntree's, everybody was there. And it was lovely to see all our work that we'd packed. And later when United Biscuits took over, they were a fantastic firm, and Sir Hector Laing, we'd do all the packing for him. Every year he invited people to go to lunch in our canteen and we took it in turns.

We'd do big displays outside our office, with chocolates, York Fruits, pastilles, oranges. It took us a long time to do all the things for the shows, everything had to be perfect. We packed the best chocolates there was. We could go even to the box store when we wanted.

I packed a box for Peter Terry and put 'Peter' in, and then packed round it. People got to know we could do boxes with '60' or '50' in for a birthday or for a golden wedding, with gold foil wrap. I even had one myself, Doreen packed it, it was our silver wedding. We did ruby weddings with a dark red foil for a '40'. We packed a lot for the Queen. She always had a two pound 1767. And when Diana and Charles got engaged, they ordered a big silk casket for a six pounder, and the same with Andrew and Fergie. When we started packing for the Queen, a man came and watched us, we had to lock the door. And we had to substitute the nuts, because there's a lot of almonds in 1767 and brazils. And we had to put different sweets in them because she didn't want the nuts in. She ordered these boxes, they weren't gifts, so we had to do them as she wanted them. They were made in Scotland. An empty casket was about 15 shillings, and when it was full it was 30 shillings. The casket had two inners in, and gold dividers that went across.

We'd only have the special packers pack these, nobody else. We had polishers to polish sweets using a little hand brush. You couldn't polish milk, it'd just go dull, but the All Gold would shine, it was beautiful. We had some lovely lids, one was Moonlight Assortment, and in gold letters it had 'Terry's Moonlight'. We still had little irons in our department, they were only about two inches long and we had to plug 'em in, we had to cellophane all our own boxes.

We'd take all the special stuff ourselves to the warehouse, in good condition. And Hazel and I were the last two in there, and then Hazel retired and I was the last special packer. The Chocolate Orange, it was a secret how much oil they put in the mixing. They used to pack chocolate for Tesco, but Sainsbury's was the best, they were out of this world.

Being a special packer, it was more satisfying, I did that job for twenty five years and I loved it. I even put a Christmas tree in a box and packed round it. Terry's used to sponsor Ebor racing, they always bought a watch, and we packed round it in a big box, for the jockey that won that race. I got a blue flash on my turban.

At Terry's they had an artesian well and they built over it with the Bindler 5. But they still used the water out of there to cool all the pans where they made the *pastilles and the York Fruits, it had to be kept at a certain temperature. They were called Bindler's, because that's the firm in Germany that made them. It's a real big machine. We always worked hard. The men used to stand around. But they got more money. A lot of them didn't like serving, when all these packers were on the belts, you'd have to put the trays in for them, and they'd shout, "I'm out of so and so, stop the belt". And the servers might have been talking or something and they'd have to stop the belt.*

In the offices underneath the canteen, they used to make their own special sweets in there. They had a little Bindler machine, to make them and cover them. They couldn't come out. We had to go in their room and pack for them. [This would be the Research and Development department – all very hush hush].

There was Spartan, Moonlight, and one called Feather. Spartan were dark chocolates and nearly all hard centres, Feather was soft centres. 1767, the two pounder, used to have cats' tongues in, a long sweet and they had cats' heads at either end. Then there was a bitter one, a mocha, and a milk in the centre. My friend used to have to count 'em in, twenty four into a box.

When we did the special boxes, we had a key to our door and if nothing was finished when we went home, we'd lock them in the cages. Forte wanted all his for Christmas so we'd cellophane them, and wrap them in brown paper with the name and address of where they were going.

They seemed to be a different breed then, even the bosses, Noel Terry and them, they treated you like human beings. Me dad always told me, "Doesn't matter what kind of job they do, you're as good as them, but you're not better than them". And even the bosses under them, Mr Milner, Mr Coward, and Mr Johnston, they all treated you like a human being. It was a lovely place to work.

During the 1960s, there were a few interesting events held at the factory. Six girls aspired to the title of Miss Industry of 1962, for a prize of £250. These were Jean Pearl, machine operator, Jean Junar, an office clerk aged 19, Kathleen Dunbar, a packer aged 25, Hazel Burrow, 19, a shorthand typist, Frankie Watson, aged 18, marker in the enrober room, and Margaret Palliser, a 20 year old sales ledger machinist. Frances Mercer, Terry's union representative, was a finalist in the National Union of General and Municipal Workers Personality Girl Competition, one of two women to be guests in London, and have dinner with Bessie Braddock and others at the Charing Cross Hotel.

Competition for title of Miss Industry 1962, for the prize of £250. L to R – Jean Pearl, Jean Junar, Kathleen Dunbar, Hazel Burrow, Francis (Frankie) Watson, Margaret Palliser.

(Courtesy Borthwick Institute)

The first taste of TV fame for Terry's had been in 1951, when a box of Spartan chocolates was used as a prop in the play 'And no Birds Sing'. But David Meek recalls a visit in November 1961 from Joe 'Mr Piano' Henderson, whose weekly programme was transmitted by ATV from the factory.

They did Sing Along with Joe. It was a good show, every Saturday night. They brought about three pianos. And he played in the chocolate mill and then while there was somebody else on, dashed down to the other end and played again. He was a very nice chap, very quiet. Apparently he started off as Petula Clark's pianist. One of the singers came down the

Sing along with Joe – Frankie Watson

(Courtesy Borthwick Institute)

overhead crane. He had a straw boater and he'd introduce the whole show. And Jim Dale came with Henderson. If they were at the Empire, they'd often come round and visit the factory. Johnny Ray came on a visit and they all mobbed him.

Three amateur singers from Terry's were in the grand finale of the 'New Voice of 1962' competition. Moira Metcalfe, aged 29, a machine operator, sang 'You make me feel so Young', Esther Dawber, aged 30, a Neapolitan carton filler, sang 'You'll never know', and Margaret Graham, assistant in the production control department, sang 'Don't treat me like a Child'.

Jim Dale 1960s
(Courtesy Borthwick Institute)

David continues,

If you had raffles for charity, they'd raise funds at Terry's like nothing, for a good cause. We had a Christmas draw and a thousand numbers. It was marvellous, I'd go into the supermarket and get 40 bottles of whisky and 40 bottles of gin. But we had a fella called Bert, he'd have loads of goes, trying to buy prizes. Then one Christmas all he won was a tin of cheese footballs. And he kicked them down the shop. And I'm not kidding you, 10 years after, if somebody said to him, "Fancy any cheese footballs?", he used to go bananas. We had another chap in the printers, he'd buy number 1, and number 1000, and I guarantee every year he got two prizes.

Addison, the works engineer, used to come in and do the draw and everybody was round then. In our heyday, we raised thousands for

New Voice of 1962 competition.
L to R – Moira Metcalfe,
Esther Dawber, Margaret Graham.
(Courtesy Borthwick Institute)

charity. And we had car boot sales in the carpark. We raised money for the very first scanner at the hospital. The women were marvellous. We'd have bingo in the canteen on a Tuesday lunchtime. You might have anything up to 400 people playing for charity.

When women got married, it was amazing the amount of stuff they got. And when they had babies, they used to buy them all baby clothes. When I retired, with us having this roving commission, [as an electrician, working all over the factory] I knew most of the people. And the amount of presents I got when I retired, it was really moving.

When I first went, all the moulds were metal. So if you went into a room where they were making chocolates in moulds, it was very noisy. And then they went onto plastic moulds. They'd keep them for years. There were all little Chinese figures and pagodas, before the war they did a 'Peking selection'. They had one Easter egg mould and it was about four foot. They'd produce this every year and give it to a charity to raffle off.

Janet Starkey started working for Terry's in the bakery at Clementhorpe in 1961.

I was finisher of the cakes. It was very old fashioned to what it is nowadays. The bakers actually baked everything, and we finished them all off next door, we did things like creaming éclairs and strawberry tarts. They did the puff pastry in our room. Our pastry used to be really nice, short pastry. We'd be forever rolling cream horns on the tins shaped like a horn. It was very interesting work, I learnt a lot.

We'd have sandwiches that would be a couple of foot long. They were made by the men in the bakery, and then you would cream them, put them in the fridge to set, and you had a big cutter like a guillotine, and cut them into squares to make into a dozen. You put jam on the chocolate ones and iced them with chocolate on a wheel, and pipe them. I'd make a special synthetic cream. We'd boil it up and put it through this machine, and it would go into the round chocolate cakes and the white cakes. You had a primus stove with a pan on with the fondant hot, and you'd dip the fancy in and hang it with a little fork while it set, then put it on to a wire, which used to take forever. And then pipe them. The big sellers were cream horns, chocolate cakes and pineapple tarts, nowhere else seemed to do them. Madeiras we did, Swiss rolls, Frangepan cakes, we'd mix the frangepan into the butter cream to make it taste. They used to sell well. Brandy snaps, I remember rolling those straight away before they got hard. Coconut buns, a pyramid with coconut and jam round.

We did spiced loaves, Sally Lunns, they were round with icing on top. Coconut rocks, they were made with egg white, sometimes with a cherry on top. When they'd do strawberry tarts and they needed a jelly, we had great big containers, and we'd put raspberry colour in, so that it flavoured. With the jam, there was apricot and raspberry flavouring and red colouring. And the Russian cakes with the raspberry flavouring. You'd save all the old bits of cake that you cut off if you were trimming and had butter cream on, and mix it up with jam and raspberry flavouring, put a piece of sponge on the bottom, a board on top with big heavy weights on, and it stayed there for a day. And then take them out and ice the top and cut them into squares, called 'Russian Fancies'.

People were very friendly. We got on really well. We were all on a big table in the middle of the room so we'd have a good chatter. It was a nice environment although we worked very hard. They were very strict, if you were laughing too much he used to knock on the window and tell us to get on with our work. But he realised later that we were still working, and apologised. You started at half seven because you had to get the creams out to the shop for nine o'clock. They'd deliver to other little shops as well.

At Clementhorpe you'd come in at the riverside with the finishing room, the bakery next door, then the kitchen. The boss's room was partitioned. We had a big walk-in fridge but it used to flood there, so you'd have to go up to the top of Clementhorpe and get in that way. The clocking in room would sometimes have a little bit of water in but we'd be walking on duck boards to get across. The men in the bakery did work hard, they started about five o'clock to get the bread done. There were three main bakers and maybe six lads, a lady washing up, and six to eight on the finishing side. You had a real variety of work. It was a lot more modern when we went up to Bishopthorpe, it seemed to be more airy.

A lot of women used to have their rollers in on a Friday if you were going out, you had to cover it up with a turban. And you used hair spray, it was the time of the bouffants really! Your hair would be that stiff it didn't move when the wind blew.

Well when I lived in the country my uncle used to bring me in his van, and when he was on holiday I'd have to cycle in, it was ten miles! I came into York when I was 18 and I had a flat. Later on my husband used to drop me off, we had a motor bike and sidecar so it was quite good fun! It was the best job, I would go back tomorrow if it was there.

We'd do the Royal Show, Yorkshire Show and Lincolnshire Show. I'd do the square chocolate cakes and there'd be forty dozen for the week at the Yorkshire Show. Mr Gee did the wedding cakes. He was fantastic at icing, that's where I learnt my skill. I did go to class but he was brilliant. He made the cake for the Royal wedding and a cake for a film with David Niven and Sophia Loren at Castle Howard. That was a dummy made out of wood and it must have stood five or six feet tall, and three foot at the bottom. He iced the dummy and he took a piece out and painted it so it looked like it had been cut, and it was highly decorated with grapes. And the one in the Castle Museum in the Terry's shop, he'd redo that when it got yellow. He used to decorate a giant Easter egg for Mr Forte every year.

Terry's restaurant 1960s
(Courtesy Mike Grimes)

Max Drucquer recalls

Peter Gee, the cake decorator. He was probably the best known cake decorator in the country. He was a superb artist in sugar. He was going to night classes and the Principal of York Art School, Reggie Cotterell, persuaded him to approach icing a cake as though it were a piece of sculpture. He really nurtured this pupil of his.

David Meek also remembers the bakehouse

at Clementhorpe, and they made the C mints down there, the Curiously Strong mints. They used oil of peppermint which is very expensive, I think it comes from America. They grow this plant, distil it and concentrate it and it's really very strong. We had a chap called Jack Holliday and you'd go in and have a joke with him and he'd throw some mint at you, and that stayed on your overalls until you threw them away. And my mother used to wash the overalls and mint was all over the house. Same as the Chocolate Oranges, concentrated oil of orange. The pastilles were down there. In those days, the girls would wrap tubes of pastilles by hand, put in the wrapper with silver paper and all the pastilles, then roll it up and they had a little glue pot to glue it. And they were better packed than when we got machines. There was row upon row of girls doing that all day long.

Mike Grimes explains,

With C mints, the process was regenerating the crystallisation of sugar. And the mint was produced from a fondant base which is glucose, syrup and sugar, which you beat, and deposit that into moulds of potato starch to produce the shape. That is then stored in a warm oven to drive off excess moisture, tipped out and the mint flavoured fondant cream, was placed into baskets and submerged into large tanks of glucose syrup. And you kept dipping these into it, a bit like making a candle, and slowly built up the crystallised sugar coating on the outside until it was the required thickness and weight. They were then drained, dried and packed. A semi soft centred mint with a crispy, candy coat, and they were twist wrapped. The Curiously Strong Lozenges are like small hard peppermints, made from a paste, and stamped out with a cutter. They were done by hand originally.

You originally cut the rings of pineapple which came in seven pound tins by hand. Eventually we started getting them pre-cut in large fifty gallon barrels. And ginger came from Australia in big barrels of syrup. Liqueurs were always produced the three weeks after the August shutdown. The spirits, brandy, cherry brandy, whisky and spirits all came in bottles, and went into the plant. You made the shell and injected, with a hypodermic needle, the measured amount of alcohol into each sweet and a little pip of molten chocolate was put on to seal it back up again. And in the flavour dispensary it was dispensed by a bloke called Charlie Druggitt [also a local dance band saxophonist] who had a special frame and turned the bottles upside down and drained them, overnight, and all the alcohol came back out of all the bottles, and it was amazing how much you gathered. In November time you'd often go to the drug store and ask for half a pint of brew, and it was the alcohol that had mixed together in these bottles. And you put it in your tea on a morning, to keep you going!

Nick Banks worked for the firm for a short period in the 1960s, in the Complaints Department.

I'd gone to college and decided that I didn't want to continue, and I found a job that appealed to me and it happened to be at Terry's as Assistant or Deputy Manager in the Customer Service Department which sounded very grand, but it wasn't. I will have been nearly 19 when I started. I was told to report to a door at the side and not to use the front doors, they were the portals of heaven, I don't think the average person was allowed to come through there. I was taken through the main hall of the office where there must have been about a hundred girls milling around, quite a daunting experience for a young lad at that time. Within the first week I was dealing with complaints. You had a standard letter for most types of complaint. And if it was outside the standard letter you went to speak to the manager who concocted one.

The majority of complaints were people who felt that the chocolates they had bought were either inedible, or they didn't like them or they felt there was something wrong with their appearance. Nine times out of ten there was actually nothing wrong with the chocolates, though in some cases the vast majority of the returned chocolates were for a condition called 'bloom', which was to do with a heat change, the dark chocolate would look as if it had got a sort of powder on it. But it was still perfectly edible, they just didn't look particularly nice.

Once I had a letter from a lady who'd sent back the Terry's Spartan and said there must be something wrong with them. She didn't know what it was but every week she'd bought these chocolates for her dog who'd devoured them. But this particular week he wouldn't eat them and she felt that there must be something seriously wrong. The standard letter went out of the window and I decided I'd make my own letter up. I told her there was probably something wrong with the dog because there was nothing wrong with the chocolates. I felt under the circumstances perhaps the dog had got sick of them and she ought to try a different brand. The letter was actually intended as a joke but to my horror it had gone missing from the post tray. I was in a certain amount of anguish trying to find out where it was and trace it. And eventually I had a phone call from the General Manager who called me in and he had the letter in his hand. He felt that I should use the standard letters that had been used and had been successful over many years, and not make up my own.

It was almost like a Victorian institution, a big rambling place, all oak panelled or mahogany panelled round the walls and corridors. You were expected to wear a suit and tie in the office and to have good behaviour and manners. If the Managing Director came through from his office, you were expected to be in attention. Be very polite and courteous and speak when you are spoken to, rather than speaking to them.

After a period of time, I was given the responsibilities of the Deputy Manager's job and if the Manager was missing, I would act as head of the department, which was quite amusing for somebody of such a tender age. I did get training in the sense that you were told the protocols to follow and the procedures to follow, and who to consult for difficulties. And you were given information about welfare and layout, and products, and given guided tours of certain areas. Then it was, 'Get on with it, and we'll check your output for a period of time'.

We had very little contact with the public other than through correspondence. The lady who was the manageress in charge of the main office, was a very strict disciplinarian. And the girls who liked to laugh and joke and giggle were soon reprimanded and told to get on with their work. But when you went into the factory, that was an entirely different situation and the girls on the production line, seeing a young lad coming in, in his suit, you were made fun of to some extent on all of your visits. The comments that were made about your appearance, and what they felt that you were capable or suitable for, was quite interesting. I used to mix with anybody whether they happened to be delivery drivers or in the factory or in the offices. But I remember the manager in my department suggested that perhaps it would be better if I spent less time fraternising with members of the factory staff and more with my own type, whatever that meant.

I suppose my first romances were at Terry's. I found it quite amazing walking in to a place where there were so many young girls who were interested in me or I thought were interested in me. I had a few more girl friends from Terry's, but everybody else in her department soon knew about your romance. So I decided that I was better off not having romances inside the factory.

I think Terry's were pretty good at that stage, in the mid 60s. They were keen to develop people and I think they did look on it as being a large family. Certainly I know from my experience of Mr Terry that he was a gentleman and always very polite and courteous and keen to see that people were in good working environments.

I think all of the confectionery firms in York had a very good reputation. But Terry's always had that air of being a little superior. And a little bit special. And certainly I can't say that I found any criticism or heard any complaints about that fact. It was always, "Oh so you work for Terry's?", as if that was quite a good thing.

I was only there about 18 months and left to join a record company. I had the offer of a sales promotion job and decided that was the bright lights, because in the *'swinging sixties', music was a big thing. I enjoyed my time at Terry's, although it wasn't particularly long. I met some nice people.*

Sandra Barnes, Anne Ruttle, Jenny Briggs 2005
(Courtesy Mike Race)

Anne Ruttle was born in 1943 and started work at Terry's as a teenager.

I lived in Bishopthorpe Road and went to Knavesmire School and just went up to Terry's one day in my lunch hour and had an interview and got the job. First of all you went as a junior to Registry then round to each department. The outside offices were mainly managerial offices. You worked your way up on whichever section you went to. I was on Orders till I took early retirement. So I worked on the same department for 38 years.

The Addressograph used to print little plates. Each customer had one. Then on Ledgers, they had a sheet for each customer. We'd have to hand pull all the orders out of the trays. I used to love this. We had pink, blue, white, yellow and green cards. Powers [the forerunner of computers] had two great big machines and they'd put the cards in, in blocks, and it would print out. We'd collect them and take them to Comps Department who checked the pricing. And if it was an error, they'd put a rip in it. We had filing cabinets with all the customers in our section. We had to find the plate and hand stamp the customer's name and address on what would come out as their invoice.

When we started it was so strict. As juniors we had to go round and collect files. There was the section head and as they finished with a file, they'd put it on a shelf. We would have to stand and actually knock on the table. You couldn't just speak to them. You had to ask if you could look through the files. And you'd never go into an office without knocking. And you wouldn't speak to management at first. Men always wore collar and tie and jacket in the offices. Over the years that relaxed. Then we got these brown overalls with a big yellow collar, with a zip up the front. They were horrible. They got more relaxed and men were allowed to take their jackets off but had to have a tie and collar. Dick Gossop, if he saw anyone speaking, he'd shout down the office, "Stop that bloody row".

It was nice at Christmas 'cos everyone was so friendly. Peter Terry would come into the office and wish everybody a happy Christmas. And the first hour we were allowed to go round each office and see all the presents. And in the latter years, they got a Christmas tree in the office. We had to cover reception and post room, and the telephones, quite a few varied jobs.

They'd have a Terry's Social, a dance every year. If we ever worked on a Saturday, which was very rarely, we liked it, 'cos we would get our lunch sent up from the front shop. This beautiful ham salad.

You weren't allowed trousers until the latter days. Nobody did really go over the limit in clothes. We had button up cardigans but you wore it back to front. It must have been a fashion. I remember some of the stars coming. The Beatles stopped me once on Bishopthorpe Road when they were at the Rialto. I told them when I went to work, and they said, "Didn't you get their autographs?" I said, "No, I just told them how to get there".

We used to have people from Askham Prison. She was really nice this girl and nobody knew she was from there. We used to save money for Christmas in the office and she said she was going home to London that weekend and she'd taken this money and we never heard any more about her. She'd taken these savings and gone.

Anne is a close friend of Sandra Barnes and Jenny Briggs. Jenny recalls,

We lived in Curzon Terrace and everybody near there worked at Terry's. If they lived round there, they worked at Terry's. So that was where I went from 1959, to '70. And then went back after I'd had my first son, in the offices part time until I had the next one, and left altogether.

My grandfather and my mother and father worked there. My mother swum the mile from Terry's to the old factory. Something that they did each year as a social thing. I'm sure grandfather also rowed as well. Years ago when my parents were there, there was maybe more going on, different departments doing things.

We keep in touch now. We meet up the second Tuesday in the month and if you're available that night you go, there can be anything from four to eight of us, all from Terry's. We go out Friday nights as well, the three of us plus some of the others are Terry's lot.

British Wool Week 1960s. Back gates at Terry's. L to R – Sandra Widd (later Barnes), Di Foster, Peter Tanner, all on bikes, model in middle, Doreen Johnson, Sue Atkinson on bikes. At back – man in tie Pat McGrath, unknown, behind model on right are Carole Botterill, Gillian ? in white, Eileen Barker, Janet Kell, Maureen Clark in white cardigan.

(Courtesy Anne Ruttle)

Sandra Barnes was born in 1946.

I started off in Registry in 1961. When you came from school and you went into that big office, there was all this activity going on and you were absolutely frightened stiff. You're so naïve. I moved eventually on to the Order Department. It was very quiet really. When that department disappeared [in the 80s] I went down to Transport Department. I was involved with getting the stock onto the vehicle, I did the paperwork, and dealing with the drivers trying to deliver when there was a tailback of trying to get there. It was all very interesting, you had to be a bit diplomatic, keep the driver calm and get the customer the product as well. I enjoyed that. Terry's was an excellent place to work.

You didn't deal with the wholesalers as much as you did your individual corner shops. Supermarkets made the whole process of moving chocolates from A to B quite heavy going, because instead of going to your corner shops, with smaller vehicles, it eventually got that you had bigger vehicles delivering in bulk. And then the wholesalers would bring their own vehicles in and pick it up straight from the factory.

They got women in the lower management side, like heads of departments. But you didn't get them going up to senior management. It was pretty much a male domain. And there was always that factory/office divide. And the two never met, only in passing. All it did was match what was going on in the outside world. You had respect for those in management and you were on a par with those that you worked with. Peter Terry was always very much the gentleman. He spoke to anybody and everybody. It was always Mr Peter. Whereas some of the management thought they were Peter Terry and they didn't speak at all. You moreorless had to doff your cap when you passed them.

I did join the Rambling Club, I was in for 20 odd years. But it always seemed to be struggling for funding.

People who've met at Terry's have tended to keep in touch with one another. It was that sort of a place. There was never any trouble that I remember. We had a one day strike. It was a lovely day and we were saying, "What a waste of time this is". And we never really knew why we'd gone on strike. I mean it sounds like a perfect place to work and it was to an extent.

When people like royalty came, they knew where they were going to walk them down, and they used to just paint that corridor and everything was spic and span. They could have blown the gaff and gone down another corridor but they didn't. They were guided down the one that had just been painted.

People were saying that Peter Terry should have never sold out otherwise it would have still been going, but there was a short range of products, and if you want to keep ahead, you've got to widen that gap. Terry's never made 'plant lines', like

Rambling Club 1965, George and Dragon, Kirkbymoorside. At far back Jerry Fortner. Back row L to R – John Worrallo, Brenda Mitchell, Bob Dodds, Janet Kay, Colin Rogers, Marion Dodds, June Shepherd, Ray Shepherd. Front – Sheena ?, Sandra Barnes, Vicky Oates, Amanda ?, Don Bowerman, rest unknown.

(Courtesy Anne Ruttle)

small bars of chocolate and tubes. It was always big boxes of chocolates, and big beautiful brocade caskets. If you've got to move on from that, then he had to sell out, he hadn't any choice.

Jean Lindsay started at Terry's when she was 18 in 1968. Her father had also worked there.

He ended up being the head of the purchasing department, buying the cocoa beans. He was really good at figures. He often brought work home and he could sit there with a bill and add the column of figures up in his head just as easy as anything. He would often go with Terry's members, fishing. They went all over the place in a minibus. He won one year, I think it was 1973. It was men only, they'd get away from their wives, go and sit by the riverbank.

I worked in the offices for nine years. And both my brothers worked there, one in the stores and one in packing. The office was open plan, with no carpet on the floor, it was all bare boards. The chairs were like dining chairs, the tables were like

Terry's Angling Club. Bill Lindsay far right on front row.
(Courtesy Jean Lindsay)

ordinary tables. There was no way you could personalise it. The office was for working, it wasn't for putting your photographs up or anything. It was strange, no daylight because we were right in the middle, with smaller offices round the outside.

There were rules and regulations and you had to stick to them. Where I work now, you can drink coffee all day long whereas we had set times and we all had to move out over to the canteen. I think there were certain times when we were really busy and you were allowed to work over but then you got a little ticket for tea and biscuits about five o'clock. I'd go to the shop where they produced the bags of waste and they'd give me the bags to take back. So people would say, "Isn't it about time you went down to the waste shop?" You could tell that they wanted some chocolate! When it was your birthday you had to buy cakes for all the girls on your section. And 'cos there was the bakery down near the gate, you rang up to put your order in. And that's the only time that you were allowed to eat the cakes. It was a good thing for them. It was well used.

Women had to wear skirts. They weren't allowed to wear trousers until quite late on. I can remember one girl came in hot pants and she was sent home. You had to be smart, whatever you put on. Every year we got a Christmas dinner paid for at Terry's restaurant and the girls all wore long dresses. We weren't allowed to go up the staircase at the front, unless you were very high up. But Noel Terry would come round occasionally into the office and have a word. That was nice.

I was doing one job for quite a while and there was another vacancy. I was the supervisor on that section for four months but then I took this post, we had to plan the loads for the lorries to go to various warehouses. I had to make sure that all the various adjustments went onto the computer and I was filling in a sheet which then went to the computer room. There was one photocopier and you weren't allowed to use it. It was the girls in office services who had trained how to use it. You had to go and say, "Can you do me this?" I think they were quite protective of it.

Industry was changing at this period of time. Work in the chocolate mill and melangeur which had always been very physical and very manual, became less so in the '60s. Some of the wheels and bogies, used to pull the pallets along, were now electric. Machines were continuously improved, more sophisticated automation came in. Germany was very progressive when it came to machinery, with some of the top engineers, and the Bindler machines were highly rated.

In July 1966, the Honeywell computer, costing £100,000, was installed for payroll, sales accounting, invoicing and stock control, as well as being able to do predictions of sales. It took up a whole glass room in a corner of the main office, as David Meek says,

> It was a gi-normous thing, almost like something out of Dr Who. When you went in, there were special mats to wipe your feet on. But now they have computers actually on the machines. At one time, if they were making bars of chocolate on the moulding plant, every so often they used to waste so many bars to make sure that the weight was right. Now the computer checks them. And if it isn't right, it adjusts the amount of chocolate it's putting into the moulds. When I finished, the apprentices were all coming up on this technology.

Charles Braithwaite did not work for Terry's but had an involvement with the company in the 1960s. He was born in Scarborough in 1929, joined the railway in 1949, and later went to York as

> Claims Prevention Investigator. I went to various companies. With Terry's, they always made me welcome.

> Terry's sent container loads of traffic to five major depots, through ADL, Associated Deliveries Limited. Three on the south coast, Brighton, Bournemouth and Plymouth, then Belfast, and Montrose. They used their own transport for anything nearer home. They sent traffic in a sealed unit with side doors and end doors. The container's owned by British Rail and is craned onto the trailer. It's over sheeted and PVC/nylon sheets over the top. It's chained on to prevent wettage.

> I could only visit the firm periodically to do spot checks. The invoicing from Terry's to the ADL managers would always be spot on. No question of stuff missing. It was in a sealed container. No-one could get into it. The main incidence of claims was on account of damage, by crushing or chafing of packages within the container or by wettage. We had to try to determine if the damage was excessive. We provided

packing frames, the old palette style, and polythene curtains to put round and tuck in. My function was to go occasionally and make sure they were loading to a pattern and ensure there was no void space. The weight of the containers was four tons. In chocolate, you'd never get anywhere near that weight. I had to analyse claims statistics to determine whether we had a higher incidence of damage on one flow more than the others.

They'd probably save damages up, have a record of which container they related to. They were on wheels and used to come back in with ordinary traffic. Their method of salvaging was to examine the outers. If the outers were simply a bit scuffed or torn, they'd take the contents out. If they were intact, they would re-outer and replace the packages, so that involved a labour cost and a bit of packaging cost. Then you'd have more serious damage where the outer was badly damaged. The traffic was either allocated to 'waste'. And the third category of damage was stuff that was so badly damaged, it couldn't be mixed in with the waste. They called it 'the swill'. I don't know whether they used it for animal feeding stuffs, but it wasn't edible as far as human consumption was concerned.

I had to ensure that the maximum salvage allowance was obtained. There was a compensation factor involved, they got paid for extra packaging involved. The Dispatch Manager, probably one of the most important men involved, was Mr Hutchinson, very nice chap. I never felt that I was a nuisance or that I was spying. I was looking to see that people handled things properly and security was okay. And if they were a bit lax, they knew that I would do a report. Terry's were as good as anybody that I ever dealt with.

At this time road transport was trying to make inroads into rail traffic, and the system of taking a trailer, putting this on, craning it on, craning it off, all the packing, it's much better to just take the lorry straight to the depots. By the early '70s, the traffic had gone to road.

I was asked to visit the firm on the 16th August 1967 relating to a derailment at Ackworth, south of Pontefract. I was called down there with two loads inspectors. It was quite an amazing sight because it was just below a little bridge. And there was the container on its side, damaged, packages strewn over quite a long distance. We had a team of rail men trying to gather up the packages, getting them back under cover in case of rain, working till it got dark. Imagine loads of bars of chocolate and loose sweets in the ballast of a rail track. The rail men were given permission, the odd thing like a broken bar of chocolate, they could put it in their pockets. Anything that was intact had to be put in security. Anything loose and contaminated had to be poked into the ballast. This was a railtrack that was going to be reopened. And the anticipation was that the local community would be tempted onto the track to try and recover some of the damaged chocolate. We left when everything was moreorless clear and we learnt the following day, the British Transport Police had apprehended a railman for theft. They'd caught him red-handed putting full cartons into his car during the night. He was arrested and brought to court. It was an open and shut case to all concerned. But due to a technicality and much to the surprise and annoyance of British Transport Police and the rail authorities, he conducted his own defence and was acquitted. His interpretation of the instructions he'd been given…everybody knew what the instruction was and how it should be interpreted but it's got to be absolute. So he got away with it. I remember the police officers were furious.

Freight trains were travelling through the night all over the country, and in my experience, this derailment and a major one at Alne near Tollerton, on the main line from York, were the only ones I was involved in. Terry's were very fair with us. I was allowed into the various packing departments where they'd been given a certain amount of salvage to repack, and one particular department was the Neapolitans, miniature bars in different coloured packs. And I'd be

Charles Braithwaite 2005.
(Courtesy Mike Race)

stood there in my overcoat and they'd put the odd chocolate into my pocket. The supervisor was quite good about it. And I was able to chat to the girls while they were working.

I had a very interesting job and to me it was the best job on British Rail. But we lost the traffic by 1970.

Lawrence Cussons, known as Lol, was born in 1928. He was known by everyone at Terry's and also became renowned throughout Yorkshire as a football referee.

My dad came back from the First World War and he was the salt of the earth. He had a favourite phrase, "Never be ten a penny like me". He thought Terry's was a solid place. It had a good reputation. I left Nunthorpe Grammar School just before my 16th birthday and went as an apprentice fitter to Terry's. I spent two years in the drawing office and then I had to go into National Service at 18 then back to Terry's. I was welding for two year. I enjoyed that. There was every kind of metal. And the lathes were there, the electricians and the fitters, it was all one shop, the bricklayers and the joiners, all at Vine Street. I did day release at the Tech College.

There was always something being done in general maintenance, because if you had a breakdown on a machine you had to get into that machine first. When I was first fitting, I was on the first floor. And there was about 16 wrapping machines for chocolates, complicated machines, all in a row. They needed two of us 'cos there was changes all the time for the various assortments. You might have to go to the engineers' shop to repair something. All the lathes and everything was down in the main shop but any minor equipment, you had in your corner. That was my real forte. I was happy doing that.

Lol also loved the sport at Terry's.

I played chess and table tennis for them. We were in the York Chess League, it was extremely competitive. I played for Terry's at football before I started refereeing, we were in the York and District League. I was also secretary of the cricket club. A chap called Vyle who was in charge of the laboratories, was a good cricketer. And Peter Terry, he was an excellent cricketer. He said about my football, "Where are you this weekend, Lol?" "I'm at Newcastle". He'd say, "Way aye man".

Unfortunately Lol had a nasty accident.

There was always a change between shifts. It wasn't a big change but it had to be done. And whilst I was working on the machine, a woman come into the room, to talk to her friend, she didn't work in that department, and she just put the switch up and turned it on. And I went right round it, I was in a devil of a mess, my thumb was hanging off, I couldn't use it for about a year. There was people fainting all over the place. They kept me in hospital for about a week and then I was off work for ten weeks then I got back to work using one hand as best I could. It was rather funny because it was then that I was going up the football ladder as well. And I'd got the best match I'd had, only on a line but on quite an important game, semi-important, you know. I said to the doctor at the hospital, I hadn't been able to referee and I said, "I've just got the best game". And he said, "I'll see you're all right". And made special

John Earnshaw, Tony Coward, Lol Cussons and Neil Ratty. 1980s
(Courtesy Mike Grimes)

bandages and everything. And I went off the field, and I could flag with one hand, it was really good. I got £750. It was reasonable then. Other people were telling me to hold out for more. I was in a hell of a state to be quite honest. The woman shouldn't have been in the damn room. And I was underneath the thing. And it was a job I did every night. Somebody should have been supervising her. It couldn't happen but it did.

It was when Lol returned that he went into management.

Out of the blue, one day they said, "We're setting up a factory at Hemsworth and we want you to go out and run it". [He was in charge of the packing]. *Just like that. But as a fitter I'd been working three nights a week overtime, 'cos I was a family man, I'd three youngsters coming up, I earnt more than I did as a manager. I said, "I can't go home to my good lady and say I got promoted, and I lost money". But they coughed up a little more and I got the company car and I got petrol allowance. But that was only with holding out. I was a member of the Engineers' Union in York, it was very strong. My dad said, "You've got to be in it my lad. You can't be an outcast". And actually there was no action, it was just like joining a club. Everyone got on pretty well.*

I was travelling every day. When you look at it in hindsight, it was very hard but I was very happy doing it. I was always on the go. They transported chocolates in bulk on plastic trays, and three or four vehicles came from York each day and went back to take all the empties back. I was packing up to 110 tons a week. The best part for me were the people, they were very good. One day one of them said, "There's two ton of coal outside our front door, if you can get it back to York, it's yours". You know, miners' allowance. I didn't take it but that was the sort of thing that happened.

There was a slight difference in wages, they were on a slightly lower rate than York but it was better than not having a job at all. They used to travel miles, even to Manchester, from Hemsworth. And they were calling all the time to see if we had any vacancies. But it brought industry that was badly needed. I had a bloke from there, saying how wonderful it was because there was no jobs there for the ladies. I had the local mayor and dignitaries thanking me for bringing jobs to the district. I said, "I am but a servant". Headlines used to appear in the local paper and what have you. We had between three and four hundred. There was a night shift as well. There was only four chaps in the place.

I was there about three years. I came back to York when the packing room manager retired, a chap called Johnny Donaldson. The Managing Director of Terry's was Ian Johnston and he says, "I want the laddie back from Hemsworth". I was sad to leave. But I had a good record and it went well for me.

All my life my approach has been I hope a courteous one. I found out, if they knew you as an honest person, they'd do anything for you. When I went there, I spoke to everybody before I started. I said, "I've come here amongst you, there's lots of things I've got to pick up. But I've come here because I like the area", which I did because I'd been there refereeing and that kind of thing. I said, "And I'm looking forward to it. And with your help we'll make it a success".

They were the salt of the earth, the people of South Yorkshire. I really enjoyed that. At that time I was in the middle of the Football League. I was refereeing Barnsley, ten miles the other side of Hemsworth. And it was a night match and so I had to go straight from work. Unknown to me the staff had made arrangements to go. I came out with the ball and one hell of a cheer came up for the referee. And they couldn't understand it, cheering t'ref before the game. And then of course the reporters got to know and next day they was dashing down to the factory to get another story.

The top floor at Terry's, there was nine conveyors, 30 or 40 on a conveyor. There was all the wrapping machines then. The actual sugar production, the centres and such as that, that was quite a conglomeration. So you'd an area manager over all that, that was part of the 3rd floor you see. And there was four altogether. There was the works manager, there was the directors and there was four area managers with brown caps.

We had a meeting every Monday to go through everything, that was the grand cap brigade. The brown caps were the ones below the works manager, the area managers. The blue for the over manager. The overlookers had a blue flash.

The Devon Milk chocolate were class. People used to talk about the class products and it's just been farmed off. I think overall the sum of the parts flogged off is greater than the whole.

I'm talking about a time when everything was in equilibrium. But from that time there was one takeover after another. And it was difficult. You didn't know who your boss was. Ian Johnston was the managing director, a very shrewd and clever man, who knew his job absolutely. I believe at times he was under tremendous pressure because the gaffers were based in London. But then you got all these takeovers. There were four in next to no time.

I finished when I was 55. The factory still went on but you got these people coming in, they had backers from elsewhere. You got on well with all your management and with everyone at Terry's, and there was some right personalities as well. You didn't make any enemies but these people coming in, the big 'I Ams', oh no. I couldn't take that.

It was people coming in who hadn't a clue about the business. The chocolate situation is unique, there's a lot of things to learn there. And people coming in who hadn't any knowledge whatsoever. What with these takeovers, there were certain people in there looking after them and they'd come in over you. And you know, they insulted your intelligence. The point is you don't work at a place like that and have a collection of a lot of experience, to have to play second fiddle to somebody who hasn't a clue is just an embarrassment. Because you can't, from the management point of view, you can't go into the chocolate industry without any prior knowledge. But that was happening. I got to the point where I really was fed up. I mean to finish ten years before your time, I never wanted to do that. But I did. At times you'd got to walk a tightrope.

From being a very happy person and enjoying the job every day that dawned, with no problems and I got on pretty well with everyone, and then when these takeovers come in, it was a different world to me. It's nice to be able to say I went to work and enjoyed every day of it and then it come to a full stop. For no other reason than people looking after other people with takeovers. Terry's was a limited company and not very long before they had the majority shareholding of 51 per cent. But to sum up, that's life, but the majority of the time I was quite happy.

Sadly Lol Cussons died in May 2009, before the completion of this publication. He was aged 80 and had been a referee since 1967, as well as a keen walker. Up to his 70s he often finished first in the annual Tang Hall walk. He sang in the choir at St Hilda's Church. A group of his friends have together bought a racehorse called 'In memory of Lol'.

Peter Terry c1963

(Courtesy Bill Godfrey)

In May 1967, it was the bi-centenary of the company and there were big celebrations. Two works dances took place on 6th and 13th May 1967 in the canteen 'To Eric Gill and his dance band with beat group'. Eric Gill was paid £30 and the beat group £12.

A commemorative ornamental fountain of early 19th century French bronze with copper bowl and plaque was installed in the gardens to celebrate 200 years of Terry's, and was officially inaugurated by the Earl of Scarborough, Lord Lieutenant of City of York, on 10th May. The pool was stocked with a variety of water lilies and golden Orfe fish.

Ian Johnston recalls organising the celebrations.

Lord Forte said, "Now Ian, what are you doing about this bicentenary? Have you got a band? What's happening when Lord Scarborough presses the switch?

Terry's Bicentenary Celebration with fountain 1967. Earl of Scarborough facing fountain, Peter Terry left of the Lord Mayor.

(Courtesy Borthwick Institute)

You've got to have trumpeters". I had an army friend at Catterick who got a band and trumpeters. And he was quite right, it just made it, 'cos the band played in the garden.

Also present at the ceremony were the Lord Mayor, Sheriff and Town Clerk, Noel and Peter Terry, Charles Forte and 81 members of staff from various sections. Noel Terry said that the combined service of those present was 3,078 years, an average of 38 years per person. All the company's pensioners were treated to a tea in the garden. During the celebrations, the guests were shown the new Bindler chocolate moulding plant, worth hundreds of thousands of pounds. This, together with new methods of manufacture being trialled and new centres being developed, heralded a new era for the company, to take it into the 1970s. A special lunch was given in a marquee on the lawn, consisting of –

Smoked trout, chilled tomato juice, Batard Montrachet 1961, then roast duckling, fresh orange salad, buttered French beans, minted new potatoes, Chateau Troplang Mardot 1959, with Charlotte Helen, Stilton and Caerphilly cheese and Dry Monapole 1961, and coffee.

Staff were given a book about Terry's and a gift bag. The Castle Museum shop was staffed by Terry's from 8th to 31st May. On 25th May, Christopher Trace, Valerie Singleton and John Noakes, presenters of 'Blue Peter' on BBC television, took viewers back in time to 1767. They visited the Terry's shop where little sugar pigs, fairy rock, damson drops, and Algerian fruits were on display. There were also Conversation Lozenges, with 'Are you in love?' and 'I want a wife' on them. All the money made from the shop was given to charity.

Castle Museum shop with three girls and soldier 1967

(Courtesy York Museums Trust – York Castle Museum)

Unfortunately, as Ian Johnston explains,

The fountain, which Peter Terry and I bought in the South of France, was stolen. An inside job I'm sure, fork truck marks on the grass I'm told.

The directors at this time were Ewart Spink, Purchasing, (who had joined in 1924 on the sales side, switched to buying in 1949 and had been in the RAF 1940-45), Harold Milner, Production, (he had joined the company in 1926 and his father Thomas had been Works Director), Peter Terry, Deputy Chairman and Sales Director, Noel Terry, Chairman, Ian Johnston (who had come from Forte's in 1964), Managing Director, Robin Terry, Projects and Services, and Robert Kenny, Development Director.

Mike Grimes, whose father was head chef at St Helen's Square,

Maurice and Mike Grimes 2009
(Courtesy Mike Race)

started work August 1967 as an apprentice engineer and I worked there for 37 years. Terry's and other companies in York sent their apprentice engineers to York Technical College for a one year training course. I was only the third who went on this full time. It was only set up in the '60s because of the government changing its policies regarding training. It gave the basic training in engineering, basics in electrical and in plumbing. Most trades were segregated. I returned to the factory, and did a three or four month period in various departments to get a feel of how the business operated, and how the engineering function worked. It was an excellent background.

The rules said that you had to have two electricians with each job because something could go wrong, and you needed the other man there to sort it out. And it was similar in the building trade. A tradesman did the work but they had a labourer to do the 'gofering'. It was a big cultural shock for me, coming from a small village into a big city and a company employing two and a half thousand people. In the early days I used to bicycle from the village at 6 o'clock to the A64, about a mile and a half, fasten the bicycle to a tree, caught the bus from Malton into York. I had another bicycle at St. Helen's Square and I cycled out to Bishopthorpe Road and clocked in about twenty minutes past seven. I must admit there were one or two occasions I've woken up a bit late at weekends, jumped out of bed, cycled to the road end, no bus, thinking, "Curses, missed the bus", cycled all the way to York, got to work awfully quiet and somebody would say, "What are you doing here, it's Sunday?" As soon as I got to seventeen it was driving lessons and I managed to buy a car and I gave the people who were on the bus lifts in to work. I remember the days when nearly everybody arrived on a bicycle and at four thirty or five o'clock it was that mass exodus, and if you were a driver you didn't go anywhere near the place, 'cos they ruled the road did those cyclists, swarms of 'em! I seem to remember eight or nine buses lining up, everybody piling on and shooting off to all the points of the compass.

You learned very quickly, particularly being shy and green as grass from the country. I remember being sent to the factory when I'd only been there three weeks, and up to the fourth floor where they used to dip cherries. I got in the lift, and there were three ladies in, we had a man who used to operate the hoist for you, it was a bit like going into a department store, like 'Grace Brothers'. And this lift stopped between the third and fourth floor, and the senior one of these ladies said, "Now then you're a new lad here, aren't you? You won't have been into cherry dipping before. We'd better just show you how we go on". And before I knew what had happened, we all wore bib and brace overalls, my bib and brace was down, my trousers were down and they got this ladle of chocolate and they poured it all over my anatomy! Then this lady, who I thought was quite old but she won't have been thirty, said, "When that hardens off come into the department and we'll show you how we lick it off". Very embarrassing for a young 16 year old. Of course when I told this to the lads back in the workshop they all laughed their heads off.

We always had tea breaks in the afternoon, and I was sent one day to the boiler-house for a bucket of steam, given a large red bucket with two brass taps on. And the boiler house was up near the factory. The engineering workshops were down near Campleshon Road in those days, three or four hundred yards from the factory. Up I went, saw the boiler-man, "Mr Jagger's sent me for a bucket of steam". He went round the back of the boiler, clouds of steam all over t'place, came back, "There you are lad". Back down to the workshop, I put the bucket up, hot water ran out of it! He says, "What you been doing? Have you been talking to them young lasses up at that factory? The steam's turned to condensation now, and it's back to water". He says, "Get up that road and get another bucket". So I went up the road, got another, back again. He says, "You'd better take a barrow with you. Don't you blooming fail me this time. You make sure you run back from that factory. I'll be watching you". And I came out and I was running down the road, and there was the whole of the engineering workshop out there cheering!

Only a week later, we were at the welding shop welding a frame up, and I was helping the engineer. They wanted me to stand on the work bench and hold up this piece of rollover section, put a spirit level on, to make sure it's nice and plumb. They said, "Make sure that's blooming lined up, if that's coming out of line we'll be right in t'cart". So they're welding away, then, "Right, that's it we've done it now", and when I let go of it the whole bloody thing fell apart, and as I turned to jump off the bench I couldn't move. Everybody used to wear hobnailed boots with steel toecaps, and they'd tack welded my boots to the flipping bench. Another day, an initiation ceremony in the blacksmith's shop, it was August, and, "Hey, you're looking a bit warm lad. We'd better give you t'blacksmith's method". There of them picked me up straight into the blooming trough, hold your head under, out you come. And these things used to go on, happened all over the factory, but within three years, health and safety, rules and regulations, stricter control on supervision, it didn't happen. Those were what everybody calls 'the good old days'.

Then I was in the drawing office for seven or eight years. I was offered the opportunity as a design engineer, and after three or four years offered the opportunity to take the role of project engineer. There were something like 33 people within the engineering management structure, ten in the drawing office, one electrical draughtsman and then project engineers brought in from outside to try and improve the efficiencies of the factory. And we ended up with a team of about 20. We designed and built our own machinery, whole moulding plants, enrobing lines. The only things we didn't build were conches, refiners and heavier engineering stuff. But small sophisticated wrapping machines were designed and built at Terry's. The time came when it was no longer economic or efficient to design and build your own equipment, you had to start going out to the purpose manufacturers, like Bindler.

When I got married, I was one of the lucky ones. I've known some of our engineers who've left the factory on a sack-barrow or a pallet truck stark naked, chained and shackled to a pallet, and just left in the middle of the car park!

The Project Engineering Department ran the whole of the engineering function. We did the layout drawing to see if it was feasible and then detailed drawings to manufacture some kit. We didn't get as much involved with the installation and commissioning, but you knew about it if it didn't fit! From 1967 I've been involved in the installation and the removal of everything within that factory, because everything has been changed.

Terry's still continued to export chocolate. Chocolate assortments went to Kuwait, fruit pastilles to areas around the Arabian Sea, chocolate burnt almonds to Japan, with other products finding their way to the USA, Africa, Australia as well as Europe. New legislation came in for exports. Chocolates sent to Canada, for example, had to have the net weight on the box, and pastilles for America had to have the ingredients listed on the wrapper. Chocolates destined for the tropics were individually wrapped in foil and carried in ships with refrigerated space.

Terry's Fitters c1930 in 'the Good Old Days'
(Courtesy Jacqueline Ake)

CHAPTER EIGHT

THE 1970s

In 1970 Noel Terry retired after 59 years service, and was succeeded as Chairman by Sir Charles Forte. It was the end of an era. Noel had initially worked in banking to give him a useful background before he joined the family firm in 1911. The following years were difficult ones and the firm struggled financially. Then during the First World War, Noel's thigh was shattered by a machine gun bullet in 1916 and he was invalided out of the army in 1918. Five years later, the suicide of his father in law, Henry Ernest Leetham, who was then Chairman of Terry's, came as a tremendous shock to the family. But apart from the period when he was Controller of the Royal Observer Corps during the Second World War, Noel had devoted his life to Terry's, being responsible for modernising sales techniques and office administration. He was also chairman of York Boys' Club, governor of St Peter's School, trustee of the Yorkshire Savings Bank and treasurer of York Civic Trust for 25 years.

Under the Forte Group, Terry's continued in the same kind of family atmosphere that had always been there, whilst still trying to move with the times. Mike Grimes was an engineer with the company.

Certainly until the early '70s, the whole production was very much a manual function, assisted by machinery. But the time came, particularly when electronics started coming in, when things became more and more automated. And you need to go down the automated route to become profitable, and, in other words, reduce your head count. Because that's where your biggest expenditure was. And that was part of our role, to source and implement automation. There'd been only two buildings erected since the originals in 1925. In 1970 they built the central services building. The canteen went on the top floor, and the next floor down was the engineering, drawing offices and management on one side, and on the other, production, with research and development and the engineering workshops on the ground floor. But that all changed again over the years. At one time part of it was turned purely into cloakrooms for everybody in the factory. They changed from outdoor clothes into work clothes, and then there was a bridge built to link the factory so you didn't have to go out into the wild world. It was to try to improve hygiene and cleanliness and stop cross contamination. In 1971 it was decided that they were moving the entire cocoa processing department into separate buildings. And we put in a new chocolate mill.

The original warehouse was still done in steel cages, and then in later years it went on to a pallet system. You deliver your product and bring back twenty pallets. It was the same as bringing your raw materials in. In the old days you would have three or four weeks' stock, but you couldn't afford that anymore. Terry's were keen to be at the forefront of technology, right through from Sir Francis Terry in the 1920s. When they built that factory in 1925 it was revolutionary.

An air conditioned unit was installed in February 1972 as was air conditioning in the restaurant, and planning permission given for a new warehouse in October 1973. As part of the York Festival to celebrate the city's 1900th anniversary in 1971, Terry's took part in the Trades Fair Exhibition at the Exhibition Hall in Skeldergate.

In 1974, the restaurant in St Helen's Square was listed as a building of architectural and historic interest. The chimney at Clementhorpe was demolished in the same year with part of the Clementhorpe site in 1975 (and the rest of it would come down in 1987). In 1975 the Terry's site on Bishopthorpe Road was designated a conservation area, along with the nearby racecourse buildings and the northern part of Micklegate Stray.

But the 1970s brought a lot of industrial unrest. On 12th November 1974, there was an unofficial strike of 150 production workers over pay claims. Maintenance workers joined them, but the strikers returned to work next day and were given the £30 a week raise they asked for.

On 7th January 1975, 300 part time workers at York and Hemsworth were laid off, and in February 20 clerical workers were sacked.

Ian Johnston

was posted up to York and became MD in 1963 right through to '82. I remember coming up and seeing the five storey block and wonderful grounds. It was quite daunting. They had splendid products, technically they were very strong, but had

been overcautious on expenditure and marketing. Across the years from '63 to '77, profits went up about 12 times. We started off in '63, profit was about £260,000, by '77 it was about £3 million. Sales had gone up several times and output as well. There were 2,600 people when I arrived, in '77 we were down to 1800. But we'd had practically no redundancies. It was natural wastage and productivity. I got on with Noel Terry. You couldn't fail to get on with Peter. There were other people who wanted to see expansion and felt a bit held back. They knew we should be doing more marketing and sales.

We were under mechanised. The chocolate enrober was 16 inches wide and you can get them up to 32, probably more nowadays. That was one of the productivity improvements but there were lots of things. But unions were a thorn in the flesh. We had strikes or threatened strikes and we had outside strikes, electricity strikes. With the internal strikes, the engineers were more of a problem, rather than the factory. They thought they had us by the short hairs. The GMU was much easier to deal with, they were more rational.

Clementhorpe was still working when I arrived, making sugar confectionery, we had a baker for St Helen's Square and a laundry on the second floor, full of steam, so you couldn't see anything. Machines were thumping quite a bit and I didn't think this was the best place so we moved the sugar confectionery to the main site and sold the laundry off. I'm very interested in archaeology and they were clearing a site to put up old people's homes and Peter Addyman [then Director of York Archaeological Trust] said, "We've found a mosaic only three feet down. I'm trying to get enough money to raise it". They needed £500 and I told Noel Terry and he gave me a cheque, and it was saved and it's now in the museum. We used to store some of Peter's artefacts in Clementhorpe. Boxes of bones and shards.

There was a wonderful camaraderie in Terry's, long service people, I remember at one of the works dances I met three generations of a family. We had a 50 year presentation. There was a picture in the corridor and a cheque. On one occasion we had a man up for 50 years and discovered that his father was a pensioner. The son was 65, the father was 95! [They were R B Pearson and his son R A Pearson. Together they had clocked up 79 years with the company].

Forte's gave a gold watch after 25 years service. Their MD rang me up, "How many people have been there 25 years?" Terry's staff stayed, whereas Forte's staff had a great turnover. So I told him 380 gold watches! I thought it was a bit old hat, it started when people didn't have watches. So I started the 25 Club, an annual party at Terry's restaurant for 25 years service, dinner and drinks and some entertainment. This happened every year. [Over 400 people would attend, and senior managers were expected to go along and show support].

We ran it fairly democratically. We were a very friendly bunch, that's why it was so enjoyable, that period. It is right to delegate and not be Johnny all things. The team blended beautifully. I was home at seven and got to the office about nine and worked hard when I was there. We only had one lot of redundancies in my time. That was when Heath introduced VAT on confectionery. It knocked sales. We had to lay off 120 people.

Watching horse racing was a hobby enjoyed by many of the Terry's staff, and in the 1970s, the firm sponsored several races, including the Terry's All Gold Ebor Handicap in 1974. On 20th August 1975, the company added £10,000, including

All Gold girls 1975. Kath Stacey is fourth from left.
(Courtesy Mike Grimes)

Terry's All Gold Ebor racing trophy 1974

(Courtesy Mike Grimes)

a trophy valued £600, towards the value of the 3.15pm race. Owners whose horses ran in that race included Clement Freud, Lord Fairhaven and Lady Beaverbrook and the jockeys included Willie Carson and Lester Piggott. Ian Johnston recalls,

A lady, Mrs [Frances] Mercer, was shop steward. She was a strong lady. When we were sponsoring the Ebor, we had a team of girls dressed in riding habits to act as stewards for our marquee and I put Mrs Mercer in charge of it. She was delighted. And the girls liked doing it.

Richard Harte started at Terry's in April 1970, and worked there until 1993.

I was working for Fortes in their personnel department, and a vacancy came up for deputy personnel manager in York. Terry's had been through the war, it needed a lot of capital spent on it and the Terry family didn't have the resources to put into it. Charles Forte needed a production site for Fuller's chocolates, so he bought Terry's.

At that time the main problem was to get labour for the factory, because the unemployment level in York was very low, about 1.5 per cent. Chocolate manufacturing was very labour intensive, and we would employ people, put them into our cream starch department, and I've known people start at seven thirty Monday morning, and they'd be gone by lunchtime, because of the conditions – chocolates had to be moulded in starch and it was very dusty. Or they'd go through an induction programme and only stay for a week or so. We had loads of problems with absence levels. Then all the employment legislation came out, so that was a headache as well. I was in personnel work for 40 years. There was no employment legislation at first, and now you can't move without it. It had to be developed and implemented. So not only were we dealing with IR [industrial relations] situations, but also various changes in running the business. And you had two rates of pay, men's and women's. When a woman got pregnant she had to leave. It seems dreadful when you talk about these things now. During the job evaluation scheme, when equal pay came in, the factors of the scheme were weighted towards men, which is all wrong, it wouldn't stand up to scrutiny now.

Retirement of union rep Frances Mercer 1975. Sylvia Brough is second from left on front row.
(Courtesy Sylvia Brough)

In 1973, '74, we had the three day week. The Heath government and the miner's strikes and the shortage of power. You had to close the factory down for three days and you had the problems of what the staff were paid, but you got so much back from the government. But it was a complete and utter mess.

When I started you could just sack someone if you had to, then legislation came in and you had to go through a procedure. You couldn't just sack somebody because they wouldn't come to work on time. You had to give them a verbal warning, a written warning and we suspended people before we sacked them. One of the biggest problems was pilfering. In those days we employed our own security people, they would hear things that were going on, or would randomly stop people and search them. And they once caught somebody with thirty years service with three pounds worth of chocolate. Well we dismissed this person, and not only did you have the unions to deal with, like APEX for the offices and sales force and GMB for the factory staff, but we also had management associations to deal with. And the managers were up in arms about us sacking this person for three pounds worth of waste. So we then changed the rules, if you were caught pilfering more than five pounds of chocolates you would get the sack, and less would be a suspension. Well it was a licence to pilfer, it was ridiculous, because five pounds worth of chocolate was a lot of chocolates, you couldn't take it out surreptitiously!

Then the rule was if you're caught twice, it doesn't matter what the value of the goods are, you would get dismissed, and we only ever caught one person twice. The chances of catching one person twice when it's meant to be a random search are very unlikely! You've got to think, "How long has he been doing this for?" Because when you catch somebody, you think it's the first time! It's not.

But I thoroughly enjoyed it. We had a company dance every year which we had to arrange, we had the pensioners party. I was secretary of the central sports organisation. At Christmas we'd have a party for all the staff with over twenty five years service, the directors' dinner every year, when the old directors came back. Certainly the work was interesting, there was plenty of variety. The personnel manager at the time was Ron Collier, and I took over from him in March '79.

Ian Johnston recalls how

we sat out a strike with the engineers by using the engineering management. It was because of the cooperation of the production staff. The engineers said the production staff couldn't even tighten a nut. There were four great breakdowns when the engineers were on strike. We got through it and that broke it. I remember on one occasion, I was asked to talk to the area secretary [of the union] 'cos we had a threatened strike. I said, "What about the people losing their wages?" He said, "We'll support the married men, the single men can wear it through. You'll break first". Like you were the enemy. They took parts out of the generating stations once, some vital parts which shut it down completely. I said, "I'm going to have the police in". Then under cover of darkness, they put them back.

Mike Grimes felt that

it wasn't just the change in production techniques and the way that management operated, we had the ups and downs of industry as well. In 1973 we were on a three day week because of the fuel and oil problems and that presented a few challenges because you can't just switch stuff off. Ten years later we hit the miners' strike, so the UK was in a depressed state again.

I was told if I wanted to work in engineering I had to join the union, much against my will. I joined the company on £3 15s. 3d a week. And then in the mid '70s, they had a 27% rise in salary in one year! Either we'd been suppressed for so many years, and they realised we better start paying these people, but it settled down again, because there was a change in the management structure, and you were treated more like human beings again. Terry's was a good company on that front and understood people's needs but there were industrial problems.

Anthony Terry, Peter's eldest son, went to work for the firm in 1977 on the marketing side.

I imagined I would do something first and then go and join Terry's. Once it had been taken over in 1963, when I was 15, I'm not sure my father found it very easy to start with. A lot of new personalities came in telling him what to do. It ran very much as a family business under Forte, but obviously when it was a family business it would have been quite different. Sir Francis Terry was brilliant, he knew everything there was to know about cocoa beans. My grandfather and Sir Francis were from different sides of the family, and ran the business together.

After university I went to a big agency in the west end of London called Leo Burnett. I was a trainee graduate and I looked after clients like Bulmer's Cider, Duckham's Oil, Perrier Water. I then moved to another big agency. I'd always been keen on Terry's and in the spring of '76 I thought it was a good time to take off and explore other aspects of the confectionery business, and I went to South America for a year and did a couple of projects. I looked at the state of the industrialisation of cocoa. Rather than sell all their cocoa beans to the UK to be processed, they were deciding that they'd do a lot of the processing themselves. The largest proportion of cocoa now comes from West Africa but the best used to come from South America. There are small chocolatiers today who still swear by Ecuador and Venezuela.

I was involved for about six weeks in Guayaquil in Ecuador. I did some more work in North Eastern Brazil where I looked at the state of the cashew nut industry near a city called Fortaleza. And so my intention was to get some experience and come back and hopefully join Terry's. After several years of advertising and marketing, this would be an opportunity especially as they didn't put a lot of emphasis on that. Under Forte there were several Terrys there. Robin Terry was on the production side and an expert on tasting chocolate. He was killed in a road accident, about December 1977, so there was just my father and myself then.

There was a management dining area. We used to have coffee there, it was very old fashioned. I remember my first day at Terry's and suddenly everybody disappeared, it was quarter to 11 and they went and had coffee for 20 minutes. I couldn't get used to this at all. But I felt it was useful to have a management dining room because there was a lot of discussion. It was useful to catch up with certain people. Terry's restaurant was still there so we'd entertain businessmen and marketing people there. We'd go down in the Terry's bright red London taxi, VY 1767. The number plate got transferred to Jim O'Brien's car, he was the Financial Director. He died when I was there, as did Doug Beacon, the Purchasing Director.

We had those very large warehouses built in the late '60s, about 100,000 square foot. They were the most modern in the country for storing chocolate. 1976 was a very hot summer and I believe Rowntree's had to use Terry's store.

There were people who could taste chocolate at Terry's and knew what was good quality and what wasn't. Bitter was regarded as being at the forefront of quality. It was very highly regarded. It would depend on the chocolate bean and how it was processed, the amount of conching. And that would have involved certain experts such as a man called Leonard Vyle. Terry's took pride in using the best cocoa beans, the Forestero bean. Now it's all very much the same, chocolate comes in tankers, processed in Belgium or somewhere.

Terry's All Gold Balloon 1976
(Courtesy Bill Godfrey)

One of Anthony's earliest projects was to be in charge of the All Gold hot air balloon, launched by Terry's. It was the world's only golden balloon, made in London by Thunder Balloons, 56,000 cubic feet in capacity, and with the registration G-GOLD. It was used for flights over the racecourse, as well as taking part in tethered inflations at Alexandra Palace, demonstration flights at steam rallies and agricultural shows. The balloon was also tethered inside Olympia and rides were given to members of the public to raise money for charity. It was the first time that permission had been given to inflate a balloon inside an exhibition hall. The most spectacular flight was the first ever Cross Channel Balloon Race in May

1978, when the balloon left Dover in early morning and landed safely near Calais. 200 numbered envelopes were carried in the basket during the race, and posted on landing. Terry's was just pipped to the post and came in second. The balloon also took part in the World Hot Air Balloon Championships at Castle Howard in 1977 and the British Championships in 1978, and made many TV appearances.

We'd go to agricultural shows and advertise Terry's in the local papers and try and get some good PR. I flew in the balloon over the Queen at York races, as well as a number of other occasions. It was involved in various promotional races. I used to go all over the country chasing after this balloon, which was actually run by a man who'd looked after our advertising, Colin Prescott. He was our advertising account executive for many years. He got his qualification for piloting it. There was another chap Robin Bachelor who was a pilot and part of the balloon company. It was a very impressive balloon.

Chocolate Orange Bubble Car 1970s
(Courtesy Mike Grimes)

They also had these little orange cars used by Outspan in the summer, and we used them in the winter.

Tony Coward got his technical and management qualifications at the London Polytechnic and worked for a London firm Lovell's. But then he saw an advertisement for Terry's,

for a sugar confectionery manager. Terry's of York was the Rolls Royce of confectionery. I was offered a job as management trainee but the first special project was to get Fuller's factory up and running. Fuller's had moved all the machinery. It was the expertise they were perhaps lacking. They opened a new department in York and put in Fuller's Lumps and Boilings Department, for peppermint lumps, fruit lumps and boiled sweets.

Fuller's didn't last very long. [Being taken over by Forte] was a good move in that it made Terry's much more professional. Ian Johnston, the Fuller's man came up and very quickly became MD of the company. We were given targets and as long as that was achieved, everything was rosy.

I did a big special assignment in the chocolate department which was very antiquated and we needed more modern equipment. I was appointed Assistant Works Manager and in 1973, Works Manager. In 1974, Harold Milner retired and I was appointed Works Director, responsible for all manufacturing, engineering and personnel at the York site. We had a good team of people. John Earnshaw was appointed about two years after I joined, he was like the number 2 right the way through. When I left in 1993, he took over the site. They were very successful and happy years. I really think we talked to the workforce. I would get there about half past six in the morning and do a whistle stop tour of the whole place, get a good feel for how it's going. And if somebody's got something on their mind, they would bend your ear. I like to think the communication was really close.

We had very few strikes at Terry's. In 1973, the time of the three day week, because of the way we all worked together, the cooperation we had with our workforce was absolutely second to none. We did have some plants on shifts but during the three day week, we worked three shifts and our output didn't suffer at all. I was involved very much with the wages. But people were asking for 50 % rise and we would say 5%. It was crazy. We had a couple of days of everyone out on Bishopthorpe Road. We did appoint a personnel director, Bob Hamilton, and he was brilliant at his job. He had a marvellous repartee with higher up unions. As soon as settlement was achieved, you immediately went back to 'Hello Mr Coward' rather than 'You Git'.

Kath Stokoe

June Holyoake and Kath Stokoe in office 1970s.

(Courtesy Geoff Spence)

went to the School of Commerce for two years when I left school, became secretary to Jack Birch for six years until I got my first child and gave work up for 20 years to bring them up. I joined Terry's in 1972 for three months, in the typing pool. There were 20 to 30 of us. Anne Shannon was in charge.

When I went back I found everything was a challenge. We started off in the great big office in the middle of the front main building. We called it the goldfish bowl because there were windows right round. We sat in rows and at the head of each row in little cubicles, were the little managers who looked out to make sure you were working hard. Then this job came up for secretary to the Works Manager, Tony Coward. I applied and in November 1972, joined him at a salary of £1,075 a year. And I had a very happy 20 years with him. He was a very good boss. I would get in, put the coffee on, open the post then at nine o'clock every morning there was a meeting of the directors so there was always something to type up for that pretty quickly.

On Friday, the Area Managers would come, each with their output for the week on paper. I had to type it all up and make sure it tallied. Quite a big job. I was always very busy. We moved over to the front offices when he became Director of Works. He would say that he was always happy when I was around, because he went away a lot and I was there to look after his interests. I did all the travel arrangements for him and others, the top hierarchy. I know today it's all Christian names but it was always Mr Coward and I made other people call him Mr Coward. And Peter Terry was always Mr Peter to everyone.

I remember the strike, they were all outside with placards. They never bothered us. We just walked through them. I wasn't in the union. In my day you never believed in it. We were all good friends, the secretaries the most. And everyone was so good at doing jobs quickly. If I wanted chocolates for samples, it would be straight over. If I wanted stuff moving out of my office, they would come straight over and do it. If Marketing wanted samples of chocolates for the brochures, I had to ask the special packers, Doreen to start with, then Sylvia and Hazel. And they would make sure that the chocolates they picked were perfect.

I was involved with everything, the warehouse, (and I believe at one time that was the largest in the north of England), the engineers, the drawing office, marketing, sales, laboratory, paintshop, garage, quality control, the office manager, personnel, security, medical, the purchase department, and the machine room where we had the computer. That's what I liked about the job. You never knew what you were going to do next. The only time I found it stressful was when we changed over to computers. I was one of the first to have one, but I didn't want to use it. I preferred the typewriter and one of the Area Managers came in. "What are you using that for?" And he picked it up and moved it into Tony's office. "Right, now you'll have to use it". And I did but I did find it stressful because in the finish I was doing the presentations for the board for my boss to present to them. A girl came through and gave us about two hours' lessons. And that was it, get on with it. The other secretaries got them, and they used to come and ask me things. But eventually *they got better than me. They were younger. And then we got another computer, completely different and you had to start again.*

I had a unique job 'cos I had so many different people coming to me. Normally, if you go and work for someone, you're just in that little sphere. All the area managers were larger than life. They used to make my day. Les Pratt was a nice chap, he'd sing to me over the phone. They all had their own personalities. I don't know whether I was lucky in the position I was in and that made a difference. I miss not seeing them, even once a year.

There was a men's bowling club next to [Rowntree's] Park. Terry's always said that they would provide another bowling green up here near the main factory. They never did but they used to pay the fees to go on the public greens. Sue from the Sugar Department and I decided to have a women's team. We asked Anita Hall, President of the Bowling Association, to come and talk to us. Harold Smith of the Sugar Department came and coached us and we got together a team and had many happy years playing in the Ladies' Evening League. The directors used to have a match with the men once a year, for a trophy. And the special packers put fresh ribbons on every year. And we sponsored the Terry's All Gold tennis in Rowntree's Park, for a good number of years. That was through Peter Terry.

Office staff 1970s. Back – Helen Standish, unknown, May Audley, Margaret Head, Marion Darby, Kay Hollis. Front – Jane Thomas, unknown, Linda Preston.

(Courtesy Geoff Spence)

Office staff 1970s. L to R – Roy Grant, Brian Chilton, Joyce Bell.

(Courtesy Geoff Spence)

Switchboard at Terry's 1970s. L to R – Stephanie Sherwood, Melody Smith, Susan Day

(Courtesy Geoff Spence)

COLGATE PALMOLIVE

In the mid 1970s, as things were going well at Terry's, the Forte Group decided to consolidate their holdings and expand the hotel side and to everybody's surprise, they sold to Colgate Palmolive who took over in 1978.

For Ian Johnston it was

an unhappy chapter. I enjoyed my Forte experience. I was very much left on my own which suited me very well. I went four times a year to London and one of their board came up twice a year. I can't remember any interference. With Colgate Palmolive, there was a culture shock. They were trying to diversify. I was asked by their man, "Have you got a phone line with a fax? My advice to you is get a shredder and connect it, 'cos you get so much rubbish from New York". He was right. I had a very efficient secretary and she came in with a telex from New York, it was 14 feet long.

They sent in a team who said, "Set out your programme", in consultation, but there was a lot of dominance. And that was what you were supposed to do for the next six months regardless of circumstance. If you stayed on that, you were the good guy, if you deviated you were making waves. Sometimes there was every reason to deviate. Our profits halved and I thought Terry's was going to fold. The profit we were returning was now less than the interest because it was borrowed money they used, not shares.

For Tony Coward,

personally speaking, it worked reasonably well because various functions disappeared and manufacturing was what they wanted, so I was factory director but this time reporting to the European boss. We had the sales director reporting to the Colgate sales man, the marketing manager reporting to their marketing guy, and the manufacturing man reporting to manufacturing. They worked everything by the book. If you did badly and went by the book, it was okay but if you did well but didn't go by the book, it wasn't good news. It wasn't a happy time, our growth stopped. They were good at selling cosmetics but not confectionery. Peter Terry was still with us, and given the title of Life President, a very good figure head but not as active in the company.

Bill Godfrey recalls,

We got Colgate who made toothpaste and golf clubs. We spent so much money in marketing that we were successful and the sales came booming in. Then they started messing about with this and finally decided, "We don't need Terry's reps. Our reps will sell Terry's".

I put on a chocolate mint crisp. We did all the usual work and research and they'd done a blended chocolate. And I decided it was too sweet. And I said it should be green. A straightforward Terry's Mint Crisp. But then the know-alls come in and you get a committee and it's discussed. And the advertising agents wanted a name, because it's easier to advertise. Then it was red when it should have been green 'cos it's mint. Elisabeth Shaw had got the ideal packaging [for their after dinner mints] and the firm that packed for them had got some agreement years ago and we couldn't get their packaging. But they wouldn't listen to me. Some things I got away with, other things you don't.

For All Gold, packaging was cheaper than any of the other assortments, because we did million runs and it made such a tremendous difference. And then with the Easter eggs, say at three or four bob, the big boys could beat us by sixpence all the time because of quantity.

I got a nice yearly bonus, so late in life I did quite well. Then Colgate decided that we must have more marketing people. And everything went through these boys. They made hashes of things and got factories to do things that they couldn't. And they couldn't understand the confectionery trade. It was a very professional setup, they ran it, they said what was to be, but still had to go outside for help, to promotion experts.

Another thing that changed the trade was women working. That knocked out the romantic era of a box of chocolates, which was great for a container of letters and knick-knacks, for fond memories. A woman who wasn't working had leisure time in the afternoon and would get the box of chocolates out. She used to look and say, "Which one shall I have?", when she was lying down and resting. [Certainly not the working classes!] The modern woman hasn't time.

There was tremendous pressure. The Managing Director referred to me as 'the stalwart of the company'. I would have been made director if I hadn't been so old. I was quite mobile and I could beat the youngsters down the stairs. When I was Marketing Manager, I said, "We can get our department in a phone box". We had a monthly meeting and the top hands would come in. I'd got a few extra people by then, eight plus the clerical staff. Then the MD said, "Bill's been empire building", and I said, "But I can still get the department into a phone box". So later I got a phone call, it was the MD. "Get the whole marketing department down into the hall". So we all went streaming down. And there in the hall we had a phone box for the staff who wanted to make private calls. So he said, "Get into that".

When I retired in 1980, [after 45 years] we had a great do.

Anthony Terry

arrived back at Terry's and lo and behold Colgate Palmolive were in discussions about taking us over. It was not quite what I'd envisaged joining. It had been run along family lines. Forte sold us for about £17 million. Colgate had been persuaded by their research people that this was a good buy. They had a small chocolate factory in Texas, with pecan nuts. So they had a little experience of confectionery but what they did have was huge marketing expertise and ran a multi national business in a way that Terry's would never have considered. They envisaged dramatically

Anthony Terry 2009
(Courtesy Anthony Terry)

increasing sales in the US and around the world with their multi national contacts. They hadn't quite understood that Terry's was a very specialised area, their name was very good but it was known only in the niche areas like chocolate assortments, Chocolate Oranges, one or two peppermint products, curiously strong mints, and Russian Caramels. A lot of cost cutting came in with Colgate Palmolive on the expensive lines, like 1767 and All Gold, and before long all the best pieces had been taken out. The whole thing was changing which upset a lot of old timers and not just the management. It was their view that Terry's were very understaffed in marketing. Bill Godfrey, a wonderful man, had been a regional sales manager and he'd been in the business a long time. He <u>was</u> the marketing department when I arrived. He reported to Ian Johnston and the marketing committee which included my father. A man called John Clackett came up, the marketing supremo, effectively dictating what the company was going to do. He'd been a Colgate man for many years. The department was growing and the workload was increasing and we had to adhere to the Colgate systems and bureaucracy. We spent a huge amount of time transferring all Terry's statistics into the Colgate format. Terry's had about 30 plus products, some of them very small indeed. A waste of time bringing in all this marketing bureaucracy for some that you wouldn't even consider advertising, like curiously strong mints, this was going on in the market department and it was even worse in the financial department.

The profitability of every aspect of the business was looked at in the finest detail. There were reviews twice a year by extremely heavyweight people, mostly American but also people based in Malaysia and we had to present to them, show them where we'd got to, and how things were developing and what our plans were. We spent half our days filling in blank books for the next presentation. It was an unhappy time for a lot of people. You felt it was like using a sledgehammer to crack a nut. The enjoyment of running the business changed completely. We only had two or three brands that we advertised, All Gold and Chocolate Oranges, but All Gold is nothing like it was and the Chocolate Orange is not what it was, all now made in Slovakia and Poland. By 1979 I was very disenchanted with it. I wanted to bring my expertise to what was an old fashioned factory with old fashioned marketing views, but I had to do it in the Colgate fashion which I didn't enjoy. It was clear to me they weren't going to find their Terry's 'Mars Bar'. I decided to leave and go back to London in 1979. I found myself flying around the world looking after British Airways advertising overseas. It was a great change for me and liberating. I learnt a lot from

Colgate Palmolive, they did have their systems and disciplines. In a marketing context it was worth learning but it wasn't right for Terry's. I felt that chocolate had been in my blood even when I was having a good time with British Airways.

Colgate only owned the business for five or six years. We'd been successful in certain markets. We hadn't been successful in America and that's where they thought there was huge potential. They would claim you only need to know about marketing, it didn't matter what the product was. Various export contracts were terminated, in let's say Germany and Holland, the Middle East and Japan. The man in charge of exports was Mark Tennyson, a great friend of my father's, his brother was Lord Tennyson. He was very unhappy with Colgate.

I was a product manager so we had to get involved in every aspect of the product. We talked to people on production lines. We'd look at new product development. The assortments changed character and the way they were packed. Everything was simplified, cheaper packaging, cheaper intrinsic materials. We really did have to put in the hours to do all the work that Colgate wanted us to do, a lot of conversion of statistics and reformatting. I was working till nine or ten o'clock at night. I would travel to London quite a lot dealing with advertising agencies and sales promotion and go out on the road with salesmen to see how the products were doing.

Of the plain chocolate assortment, All Gold was 20% of it and if you included Moonlight our milk and plain assortment, we would have been one third of plain chocolate assortment, and Rowntree's Black Magic would have been probably a third [nationally].

They came up with the Chocolate Lemon. They were very keen on line extensions and Colgate were keen on lemon because they used it a lot in soap. We didn't think it tasted as good in chocolate. You get a lot of flavours today like lavender and even chilli in chocolate. But it only lasted two or three years. We did a lot of small lines, and a lot were got rid of, very fine products like curiously strong mints, and Russian Caramels.

My father loved talking to anybody. Great for morale and for PR. My grandfather was totally different, a quiet man. He had his interests, one was conservation, the York Georgian Society and the York Civic Trust. He was very benevolent and left a lot of money to do good things in York. I recall it being a very happy place before I joined. I joined at the worst time, we were all under tremendous stress. I learnt a lot but it wasn't a great deal of fun.

Ian Johnston recalls that Terry's started to do

television advertising. We promoted Chocolate Orange. When I first knew the product we were selling three tons a week, we got to 70,000 tons a year later. We got a Volkswagen and got a firm to make an orange body for it, enclosing the driving seat. It just looked like an orange. There was a table in the back and you could have customers in and proper demonstrations. We had a very good advertising agency, Coleman, Prentice, Varley. From the mid '60s on, we got quite seriously into advertising All Gold, Chocolate Orange, Devon Milk, Neapolitans.

Moulding became more important in that period, with the Bindler, a very good German machine. The supermarkets did not dominate the market as they do now. We were selling a large part to CTNs, [confectioner's, tobacconists' and newsagents' – basically the corner shop], part of their raison d'etre was the range. We were all for expanding some of our lead products, and Christmas boxes and Easter eggs. I thought the lesser breeds were good support products. The Curiously Strong Mint was the oldest recipe in Terry's, from 1860. We had a good margin, it wasn't getting in the way, wasn't taking up too much space. And there were other products like plain and bitter chocolate, they were well regarded. [But Colgate Palmolive dropped a lot of these]. Product development was done in-house. Waifa and Chocolate Orange and All Gold go back to the '30s which the Americans and Colgate couldn't understand. It was getting very much harder to think of a new line.

[Before Colgate Palmolive came] we did new training but didn't go in for all the management brainwashing. I'm a bit sceptical about these courses. I think the first thing was primarily to increase productivity. We bought a better plant and introduced a work study department and the computer made a great difference to the administration side of Terry's. We had a new big air conditioned warehouse. Our expenditure was self financed. We were generating enough to support the programme we were running. In '77, interest rates were very high, about 14 per cent. It was absolutely the best part of my career. I had such a nice team, we got on so well and we were successful.

The marketing people didn't always get it right, as David Meek recalls,

The Terry's Bitter bar was absolutely delicious. Even in those days it was a very expensive bar of chocolate. The Oliver Twist bar was just a little bar with a photo of

Oliver saying, "Please sir, I want some more". Then they decided it was a bit old hat, so they just renamed it Terry's Dark and the sales dropped to nothing. So they went back to Oliver Twist and it went up again.

Ian Johnston realised that much of what he and his team had achieved between 1963 and 1977, increasing profits twelve fold, was beginning to unravel under Colgate. Profits fell so steeply that people were genuinely worried.

I told Colgate we were proposing to up the storage capacity [for the computer]. Then I got an answer, "No we're going to link you by cable to the computer in London which is also Honeywell". I didn't much care for this because Terry's was freehold, with plenty of space to enlarge the computer. I suspected and was proved right that our traffic was more than 50% Colgate UK. But they pushed it through. They had a chap in New York who had the final say. And a year and half later, we were presented with an increase in rental of £250,000. I queried this and was told it was a rent review in Oxford Street.

I got a little team together and planned and plotted, mostly in my dining room at home. We had to keep it under wraps until we knew whether we had a runner or not. We had a merchant bank helping us and a lawyer, it was very much an inside effort. I needed a code name for secrecy so I produced LOHAG, Land of Hope and Glory. I was trying to repatriate the company from American hands so it seemed appropriate. The other runner was United Biscuits. They could bring in synergy, [including separate distribution and computerisation]. It did give them savings which a stand alone outfit couldn't produce. I discovered afterwards if you took out synergy, our bid and their bid were within a few thousand of each other. At least I got it into British hands though it didn't last. We had a very sound plan. I don't think we expected the supermarket factor to be as big as it became. We were going to buy one or maybe two sugar companies to widen the Terry's sugar side 'cos it was predominantly a chocolate company. There would be economies of scale in doing that. We were going to get rid of a lot of what we thought was wrong spend by Colgate.

I went to see Lord Forte at the time. He said, "I'm not going to put money in, but you've certainly got my blessing and you can quote me. And if it doesn't work, I want you back". I think I was a team runner, I enjoyed leading a team. None of us knows whether it would have worked but we would have tried hard.

John Earnshaw was one of the LOHAG group. He had come to Terry's in the late 1960s at the age of 18.

> I had to go to Leeds Metropolitan University and took professional examinations in the Institute for Work Study Practitioners. Quite taxing when you're working as well but I enjoyed it. We had to persuade our bosses to allow us to go on a residential as part of the course. I had to see Mr Milner to persuade him that it was as cheap to go to Spain as it was to go to Scarborough. He was very good, and just before I went, gave me a £5 note and said, "Enjoy yourself while you're there".

> I developed my career through the work study stream to start with. I liked the atmosphere at Terry's but I was ambitious to move my career on. Then they offered me a role as Special Assignments Officer, we called it 007½, developing the warehouse, big building projects, and new line extensions. In 1976, I was offered the role of Work Study Manager. It wasn't many months after that we were acquired by Colgate Palmolive. And I found myself being interviewed for my own job by an American guy that I'd never met before. And I was re-appointed to the role. Terry's was very traditional, and some of the administration and finance that was available was not particularly sophisticated. And they [Colgate Palmolive] did have good, strong financial, operational and marketing skills. And they brought it all together, and said, "This is what you're going to deliver". But the Managing Director, Ian Johnston, wasn't involved in the discussions and yet he was the one responsible for delivering the outcomes! Then Colgate changed their chief executives. And for about a year we were left just drifting. We had no direction, no capital. Ian called me down and said he was thinking of trying to execute a management buyout. And there were six of us in the end who spent the best part of a year to develop a business plan and to try and finance it. I was the junior one of the six. But my financial background was strong enough to be able to do that. Ian wanted to bring Terry's back into British ownership. And it was good fun, we had a year working with outside people and investment bankers and it was the best training that I ever had. We worked on Saturdays, Sundays and evenings. I think a few people were trying to guess what was going on but never got to the bottom of it. And we got to the stage where we offered to buy the business. We raised £17 million but in the end they took £25 million from United Biscuits [in 1982]. What United Biscuits did effectively was to buy the goodwill for £8 million. But UB allowed us to develop the business plan that we'd put on the table to Colgate Palmolive.

Peter's father Noel Terry was a very strong character. But when the family sold out and Forte took over in '63, they effectively gave control to somebody else. The person who had the greatest influence in my early years, was Ian Johnston, a very strong character.

If we'd taken over, I don't think we'd have been able to develop the business sufficiently without additional funds, we'd have had to sell on. We thought maybe three to four years. And in a way that's just about what United Biscuits allowed us to do. We'll never know whether it would have been better or worse.

In 1980 Kathleen Terry, Noel's wife, died aged 87. A lady called Mary helped to nurse Noel at Goddards before he died later that year.

One of the nurses had once been the Terry's maid when she was fourteen. She got married when she was 21 from their house and went in a posh car and the reception was back at the house. I'd work there [at Goddards] all day, but I'd do nights when there was nobody else. We'd have our breakfast, he always wanted toast and sardines grilled with margarine on top. He had a really big dining room table, it's now in Fairfax House, and everything carried had to have one of these silver tops to keep them hot. For lunch it would be stews and jacket potatoes, and the table would be all set with beautiful silver. He only liked simple food. His sandwiches had only to be an inch square, so you had to cut crusts off. He had an electric fire, but in the old days there'd be a great big fire. And he always had Terry's waste chocolates in a bin at the side of his chair. He used to give us a big Easter egg, Peter Terry would bring it. There was an attic the whole length of the house and it was full of antiques. I know there were these old fashioned cameras that pull out, and glass negatives. The staircase was as big as those at Harewood House. They had a gardener who lived at the coach house, Seth. And he'd been there 28 years, and he was allowed to live there after the National Trust took it. Everybody had to be a nurse, because if he collapsed you had to know what to do. There was a phone in nearly every room, and he had a bell! We used to do his washing, and Peter, if he was going to a function, would bring his white shirt, because he was at the factory every day, he'd say, "Can you just iron my shirt, make it nice?"

I worked there for five years, then I left, but they sent for me the week before he died. "Mr. Terry is needing to have injections and none of us are allowed to give him one". He was very humorous, and a great man. I've still got a letter thanking me, with a poem about me.

In July 1980, it was reported that the restaurant was to close after 150 years. It was purchased by the adjoining Trustee Savings Bank in October. A two day auction of fixtures and fittings took place in December and included such items as mahogany Adam-style tables and chairs, teapots, silverware, kitchen utensils and table linen. It raised £30,000.

It was a Grade II listed building, on the original site of the Praetorian gate of Roman York with an Ashlar stone façade with Corinthian columns, marble stairways, mahogany panelling and richly decorated plasterwork. The building included a basement with cloakrooms and lavatories with marble floors and walls, the boiler house and several cellars. On the ground floor with its marble floor and show cases, were the restaurant with its ornate ceiling and frieze, fitted bar, and ante room with catering hoist, and the kitchens, chill room and deep freeze.

The first floor with its elegant staircase, led to the café and the ballroom which had three French windows with wrought iron railings and floodlighting, then the still room with food warming and chilling facilities, more cloakrooms, chef's room, staff room, and butler's pantry. The second floor housed the oak panelled Tudor Room with Minster stone fireplace. An annexe had a doorway leading to the bridge link with the insurance building at number 1 St Helen's Square, and there were also another kitchen/washing up room, flat roof area, and prefabricated equipment store. Next door was the small Georgian house, home to the Terry's in the 18th century, later used as offices.

Although the restaurant closed, Maurice Grimes, with another chef, stayed on to honour the Christmas bookings. Many people were not happy when the catering side of Terry's closed. But their feelings did not come into it as Mike Grimes explains.

Colgate Palmolive couldn't understand why a confectionery company ran a restaurant and outside catering company, couldn't get their head round it. They just thought, "It's a nice lump of real estate, they've been knocking on the door for 50 years trying to buy that place".

But John Earnshaw had to do a study on it.

And it was an absolute disaster when you looked in reality at what was happening. I recommended that was closed because it wasn't profitable. The front shop wasn't profitable either and a lot of management time was going into it. Colgate were saying, "You should not be in this game". The outside catering was probably the only thing that was substantially in good order but without the front shop, it couldn't really exist. There was probably three quarters of a million on the table for the front shop. It was a lot of money and in effect that was going straight to them. But it wasn't making money, and there was no real prospect of it doing so.

Fred Thomas had started work at Terry's as a baker in the late 1970s.

John Johns was the foreman and Peter Gee the manager. We had about ten altogether. Terry's bake-house was really clean, it was quite big for the size shop we had. I was doing the mixing at one end, with Hobart mixers, a proper weighing up room and a store room. Further on was the big sink and two big reel ovens, ovens with shelves that go round slowly. Then there was a big prover which we put the racks of bread in to rise. We made some really nice cakes, and bread, all top quality. But Terry's didn't really change with the times.

Fred Thomas 2005
(Courtesy Mike Race)

[They could have got] a high speed mixer, and a dough retarder, it's for where you can't get anybody to come in early on a morning, so you do it on an afternoon, and put it in a fridge already moulded up, and the fridge turns itself on early morning, from a fridge to a prover with steam and heat. When we go in on a morning it's ready to go straight in the oven, so that does save a lot of time. We supplied so much of the stuff to the canteen, but the canteen made their own little scones. We sent bread cakes and sold cakes to the factory workers, we had a little shop.

We used to start at six o'clock, but on a Friday we'd start at midnight, to get the bread done for the front shop. They didn't do a lot of bread really, because we used to buy it in but we'd make wholemeal bread, white bread, a lot of bread cakes and dinner buns, crusty cobs and Vienna. And Terry's lunch loaves. They were special in the way we mixed it, and the way we put it in a tin, and just let it come to rise. I've been a baker for quite a few years and I've never seen owt like it. The mixing started off as dough, we'd let it rise for about an hour, till it came to the top of the mixing bowl, then we'd mix sugar and margarine in, and beat hell out of it until it was binded together, and it was really sticky, and you put the fruit in it. There was as much fruit in it as flour. Then we cut it, scaled it off, moulded it up and chucked it in the tins and it used to come out lovely every time. A lot of 'em put bread improvers in, but at Terry's we just put normal lard in it. Terry's stuck to the old fashioned recipes and methods. Swiss rolls we did, and fried doughnuts, and that's the same mixing as a teacake mix with no currants in. We'd do the tea cake mix first, and left so much out for the doughnuts, and fry the doughnuts into different shapes and star signs, then bake. They had a big rack where I was weighing up, all these bowls weighed up for the rest of t'week. They had cheese scones mix in one, fruit scone in another, bread in another, and loads of bowls all weighed up, but that was the way they used to do it. It was fairly unique 'cos there was more room to work, it was a bigger place to where I'd worked before. The mixers were in the middle of the bakery, and you could walk right round them.

At the restaurant in St Helen's Square they used brown bread for side salads with prawn cocktails. So about 36 small loaves of brown a day, and quite a bit more on a Saturday. I was also chef-ing there on a Saturday night for a bit of pocket money, and I went to Scotch Corner once to cater for a big wedding. I could see what they was buying in, what we could make. It was a really nice place. The ladies and the waiters, we had good team work. I was doing the cooking – steaks, fish, starters, soups, anything they wanted. The restaurant was a lovely place to go to. We could get up to 50 people for high teas till about six, and then it would change to a restaurant, and I could serve another sixty people, depending if they had any parties coming in. It was mainly downstairs, and upstairs was like overflow.

And then the waitresses, they usually do the starters and the soups and that, and at t'end of night they used to wash up. Well I started doing all t'lot, instead of me stood around waiting for them to do the starters, then start the steaks or the gammons or anything else, I started doing everything and we got great team work going.

It would be steaks, gammons, all garnished either with chips or vegetables. The sweets was all prepared, you know, the gateaux and that, they were all to one side, what ever they wanted, but the girls used to do that.

And we'd supply wholesale orders. They would come from these little shops in York, to the back entrance. While we were working these big ovens it was easier and better to fill them than to half fill them. They made a hell of a lot of cakes; fondant dips, which is fondant poured over a bit of sponge. They made chocolate cakes, square ones, they were lovely, they were finished off really nice, and they went all over the country with them. They used to go to the Yorkshire Show, and we used to send a lot of cakes. They used to cater for weddings and parties. The wedding cakes, that was a special mix. I've never seen owt like it. It was steamed first, like a Christmas pudding, then it was baked. And the cake was lovely.

Now you do it all out of one mixing, for baps or bread cakes, it's just different shapes, the moulding. Years ago at Terry's they'd do all these little recipes, just for one item.

When it closed it was a really sad time because the bakery could have gone on and on, and done more wholesale, even if the shop shut down.

Fred now has his own bakery on Albemarle Road.

I've carried on making Terry's cakes, as much as I can, Terry's pineapple cups, lunch loaves, paradise slice, with a pastry base, with lemon curd. The mixture is ground rice, ground almonds, fruit and eggs, no flour. And that's a nice mixing.

It was a good place to work, at Terry's, I enjoyed it. If they'd been still open now I don't think I would have left. But [a part of] Terry's still lives on, through me doing their cakes.

CHAPTER NINE

THE 1980s AND UNITED BISCUITS

It seems that the Colgate Palmolive days were not happy ones for Terry's, but that things improved when United Biscuits took over. Ian Johnston was asked to remain as Managing Director but decided to return to Forte and was replaced by Bob Clarke. Hector Laing, who was knighted in 1991, was the Chairman of United Biscuits.

Hector Laing of United Biscuits 1987.

(Courtesy Mike Grimes)

Betty Hartas reflects,

Colgate Palmolive came in with a bim and a bang and they sorted this and that, but they didn't replace anything. They took it right down to the very bottom. And when United Biscuits came, Sir Hector Laing said it was the 'jewel in his crown'.

Kath Stokoe

didn't think soap and chocolates mixed. When Mr Johnston left, my boss [Tony Coward] was then made up to the top man over all, reporting to United Biscuits chiefs. So we went to a big office in the front building. I was in contact with United Biscuits by phone, and they came visiting quite a bit. I liked meeting all the different people, they were a good crowd. It was part of your job, to know what they think and do. I'd get to know if there were any problems. When Colgate Palmolive were there, there were always leaving do's, a lot of activity going on. I've been to dances at Terry's in town and I remember conga-ing round the square one day. Don't know what the Lord Mayor would have thought.

Personally, I thought Colgate Palmolive were asset strippers. There were about 2000 there when I started, but by the time I finished, it was really well down. But United Biscuits brought my wages up. At Easter we'd get a whopping Easter egg. I was on the taste panel for a little while. Anything new that came out, I'd get a taste.

Tony Coward explains,

It was a real growth period with United Biscuits, they got us into own label making products for Tesco, Asda, Sainsbury's and Marks and Spencer's. They made a huge investment in the company. We built a new chocolate manufacturing area. The best relationships were with Sainsbury's and Tesco. They are pretty loyal to you. We made mega tons for them. So the volume went up from about 700 tons a week to 3000, through mechanisation and different products. Chocolate assortments nearly disappeared and Chocolate Oranges grew and bars grew. Chocolate Orange went from being hand done to being totally mechanical.

Tony Coward.
(Courtesy Mike Grimes)

Originally we bussed people in from Hemsworth, then we moved there and built an extension. But in 1983 I had to go out and close the factory. They had been so good to us and an absolute lifesaver, but it just didn't make sense there so we had to close it. It was the worst thing I had to do in my working life.

The market changed. People [stopped taking] boxes of chocolates [as gifts], but would give flowers and wine. And there was the obesity thing. So the assortment market went pear shaped. United Biscuits formed a division called Terry's Group, then took over Callard and Bowser, [who made high quality toffees and butterscotch], *Nuttall's, Smith Kendon travel sweets, Chocometz in France and one in Italy,* [also Verkade, a biscuit and confectionery manufacturer in Holland]. *I was on the acquisition team and I became Group Manufacturing Director. I spent a lot of time in aeroplanes going to London, Bridgend, France and Italy. Those were really good days. I like to think my strength was delegation. My style was definitely democratic. The buck stopped with me but I would listen to what they all had to say.*

1970s factory staff. Back L to R – Bob Tomlinson, Darren Grey (son in law of Vic Botterill), Steve Wiper, Tony Otto, Matthew ? Front – Jean Airdale, unknown, Josie Black, Jenny ?, Margaret Wilson.

(Courtesy Geoff Spence)

Terry's shop L to R – Joyce Gee, Ethel Doran-Thorp, Sybil Mason.

(Courtesy Geoff Spence)

Preparing fruit pastilles. 1980. (NB the man watching the women work)
(Courtesy Bill Godfrey)

Richard Harte describes the last days of Colgate Palmolive.

We started to get lots of labour problems, a hangover from the three day week. Our rates of pay began to slip behind Rowntree's, particularly fitters, and they were the ones who became much more militant. Terry's had never had to deal with anything like this before. They got rid of the front shop, which was a big concern and people were very unhappy. And there was a sudden downturn in trade, and we needed to downsize, so we had lots of issues. It was a stressful time, a lot of negotiations. We had our own building department, our own draughtsmen, drawing office, development engineering department, builders, painters and carpenters on site and it was decided that all these things could be contracted out and that the main thing was to manufacture chocolate. But of course that meant redundancies.

In the '80s we had contracts with Marks and Spencer's, and the big supermarkets. Colgate's philosophy was if you can manage one business, you can manage any business. And it was the fashion at the time to diversify. But they were very bureaucratic, they'd send teams in to look at the business and go through it with a fine toothcomb and use the same format to audit our factory as they would with a soap factory. When United Biscuits bought us in 1982, it was the finest thing that ever happened to Terry's, they were very good employers. They bought us after we'd been through this restructuring, and then we had to conform to the United Biscuits format, which was slightly different, So we had the York factory and a factory in Bridgend in Wales.

Sandra Barnes believes,

To sell to Colgate Palmolive was just stupidity really, 'cos they were trying to put chocolate and their products onto the same vehicle. United Biscuits invested money, improved it a lot and made it a nicer place to work. United Biscuits were taking over the computer side. It was only when I went to the Transport Department that we got any sort of computer knowledge. And United Biscuits said, "We're here to stay, that's it now".

As the workforce lessened, you were supposed to take on more work, to encompass the jobs that had left. You had to be multi-skilled. To a certain extent you get in a comfort zone and you know the wages are there every week so you stay where you are. But you just liked going to work, and that's a big thing. The fact that we all keep in contact with one another is a good sign.

Mike Grimes describes some of the changes.

Until the mid '70s, the whole production was very much a manual function, assisted by machinery. But things started becoming more automated. Our role was to source and implement automation. But that takes away the opportunity to be flexible. They needed to be on the production 24 hours a day, seven days a week, and ideally on the same product, because that's where the profitability is. Colgate Palmolive only lasted five years and they brought down St Helen's Square, and the outside catering business. The good years again were with United Biscuits, a British owned company who had the vision of innovation and the development of new products. We had an in-house Research and Development department that plugged away trying to come up with new ideas.

Most of my working life I thoroughly enjoyed, I enjoyed the people, the companionship. Everybody has ups and downs but they were far outweighed by the good times we had. It was bliss.

Betty Hartas was still working in Personnel but also helped with doing promotions.

I just loved it. If it had been possible in my day, I would have liked to have been on the road selling. And I could have done it. But you didn't have ladies on the road.

The company entered a float in the annual Lord Mayor's Parade several times in the 1980s and Betty organised it. In 1984 they had a replica of the Terry's shop from the Castle Museum, and staff were dressed as employees through the ages, from 18th century times to the futuristic space age.

Betty Hartas and Benny Lister,
Lord Mayor's Parade float
(Courtesy Betty Hartas)

Lord Mayor's Parade. Betty Hartas and Shirley Turner.
(Courtesy Betty Hartas)

Richard [Harte] *said that we could go into York to some amateur group to borrow the* [Victorian] *dresses. But we didn't like them. I said, "What about going to Homburg's in Leeds? I can ring there and get a driver and take us". He said, "We can't afford that". But we got a chauffeur and a car and went to Homburg's. So I got the owner, didn't I? And we tried dresses and dresses on to get ones we liked. On the Monday they had to be returned. So I went down to Dispatch Department and picked the biggest box of chocolates I could find, got it packed up with our dresses and sent it back. We told him what a wonderful show it had been and that the gowns were beautiful. And we never did get a bill!*

Sylvia Brough recalls another reason to admire United Biscuits.

They used to have 'shepherds'. David Meek was one, he was a lovely lad, Lol Cussons was, Bob Brainbridge was, and every year they would take pensioners a parcel of biscuits. And they'd go out and see if the pensioners were all right.

Pauline Bradley began work at Terry's in 1950, although she had a break for some years, but she had to wait until 1980 to get promotion. In the early days, women as managers were unheard of. She recalls her first day at work.

I was absolutely terrified. 15 year olds then weren't like 15 year olds now. I think I still had ankle socks on. I remember standing outside these doors until someone said, "Come in". They were mostly women, but men pulled the loads of chocolate away. My job was on a plaque machine. They came from the enrober room full of chocolates, were taken to the packing room, came back empty, and one of my jobs was to tip one on top of the other, they just clicked in. I was in Production Control.

We held a stock of about 300 spaces, each marked with a number, and you would put Russian Caramel, and the next might be Raspberry Trifle, or Coffee Cream. And you'd check and if you were low on one, I'd order some more, but if somebody got tickets in the wrong place, we'd got loads of Russian Caramel but no Raspberry Trifle. If 200 packers are going to be sat waiting, there's hell to pay!' So you had to get it right or it could stop the factory! You couldn't send out a box of All Gold with one Russian Caramel missing. Then eventually when the computers came in, at the touch of a button you knew how many there were, and where they were.

I was there when sweets were rationed, we had coupons, and we had a shop where you could get things. A 'D' coupon was two ounces, and an 'E' was four, and we had to take coupons off people. I got a job in the office as a clerk, and I got to senior clerk. And then my boss left, and then later they asked me if I wanted the job. I was the only female manager. There were four men and me, brown hats, area managers. I always wore trousers every day and when I got this promotion it was like a French Foreign Legion thing I had to wear, with brown round, [a kind of cap] and I thought I can't wear trousers and this thing on my head as well. Then they all said, "Ooh she's got legs".

You cannot beat factory workers for helping. [For anyone having a baby], they would get the pram, the cot, baby clothes, everything. Even if they were married, but mainly these girls who got into trouble, they'd buy them everything. There was a fantastic camaraderie, you'd make sure they weren't struggling, the girl wouldn't have any expense for the baby until she was on her feet. Factory people like that are really, really generous.

When Pauline became a manager, a blue hat, she had thirty employees under her. The Jubilee Times for February 1984 read, 'Pauline Bradley has been appointed head of Production Control Department. She is only the second lady to head a production department at Terry's. The first was Elsie Millard who managed the Enrober Department for a number of years'.

It wasn't that I was brilliant. I could do maths, and I knew the job inside out, right from scratch. I found out that the staff, if you treated them properly, would do anything for you. But one thing I had to watch was clocking in and out. The girl who worked with me, we were friends from infant school and one day her sister came, to clock her in. I said, "You clock her in and you can take yours and clock out, and I mean it, I'm not joking". And I thought, how dare she? But we were such good friends she didn't get the huff. And stealing, Terry's were very lenient with you eating sweets, but no stealing. But they'd take all sorts, anything they could get out, they would take.

I was there on a Saturday morning and I was there at half past six on a Monday morning before they came in, and my office door was open, and they knew they could come. One girl, the overlooker said, "She's sat on her backside and she won't pull this work". So I sent the two clerks out and she came in, and I said, "What's the problem? What you tell me, that's it, finished". She started crying, and she'd had an abortion. So when the overlooker came in, I said, "She's not well, and until she's well again, she can sit there. I don't want you hassling her". I thought there was no way she could be pulling those great big things, they weigh tons. She needed to come to work, she was a good time keeper, never been in trouble before.

I was the highest paid woman. When I left, I got tables and tables of presents, and the bosses took me out but it was sad, from going in at 15 and walking out through those gates at 52.

George Bradley is Pauline's brother in law. He worked at Terry's from 1983 to 1994. He recalls how things had changed from earlier times.

I was sent to Thomas Danby College, a college in Leeds, with a laboratory, because I knew a bit about chocolate. They showed you how to do chocolate moulding. With the Chocolate Oranges, there were two men at one end making sure the chocolate's flowing all right, the oil was going into the chocolate, and producing the slices. One bloke used to put the plaques on the machine and there'd be a bloke at the end. You had to pick them up in tens all nicely on top of each other, and put them on a pallet, turn them different ways and put a ticket on.

They were put on bogies and taken away to the lasses on the machines to wrap them. Because I knew about chocolate, I went on to the Waifa machines, and of course it was automation then. But it would break down sometimes, and get blocked. When I was finishing, the Waifa was going, and the Orange all went on automation, and they stopped all them lasses, all the lot went. [Eventually 'robots' were actually producing the chocolates].

In the later years I had a bit of a 'tache and a beard, and had to wear a snood. I'd be cleaning, and I couldn't do with it on and Richard Brown would say, "George, your snood". And I went bonkers one day, and said, "You go down there and smell the smoke on the end of that machine. Go into that smokeroom and tell them all to stop smoking, and then I'll put my snood on". He says, "I can't do that", so I says, "I can't put a snood on then". And he didn't do nowt about it. And the smoke room door was opening and shutting all the time, and when you walked along, the smoke went straight into you as you walked past. He couldn't stop them smoking, and there was more chance of smoke coming out of that room than my beard!

Visit of Margaret Thatcher 1980s. John Smyton behind her. L to R – Madge Beard, unknown, Pat Yates, unknown, Max Dodd, Adrienne Hope, Ian Bruton.

(Courtesy Anne Ruttle)

In November 1985 the firm announced that profits had increased by 75%, and that they had won an award from the Institution of Marketing. They were to launch new products in the spring of 1986 to try to claim a bigger share of the market. Peter Terry, the last member of the Terry family, retired in December 1985. He was still very busy, and was on the committee of Fairfax House, supporting plans to restore the property and display his father's Georgian furniture collection. He was also Chairman of the Noel Terry Charitable Trust, set up to support groups in the city, and was involved with York Civic Trust.

The Imperial Group planned a takeover bid for United Biscuits but dropped their plan in February 1986. Construction of a new £5 million liquor plant began in April 1986 and was finished by May 1987. It measured 40,000 square feet. United Biscuits had chocolate refineries in York, London, Glasgow, and Liverpool and rather than have four new sites, all the latest machinery was installed in York for bean cleaning and blending operations. Eight tonnes of beans could be cleaned in an hour, and one tonne roasted in less than an hour, with a capacity to produce 10,000 tonnes a year. A workforce of 1,370 was now involved in manufacture, this was an average over the year to include seasonal workers. There were still three types of chocolate, the standard plain, plus bitter and milk. There were straight lines like Hazelnut whirls, truffles and Turkish delight, plain and orange bars, fruit and blackcurrant pastilles, crystallised peppermint creams, sugared almonds, and specialised supermarket products. The beans had stringent checks made, with various examinations for suitability and to see if there was rancidity or moisture. Then there was metal detection, and further cleaning by highly sensitive machinery to remove string and paper. Six to eight varieties of bean were used, from West Africa, the West Indies, South America and the South Pacific.

In 1987 national sales of confectionery topped the £3 billion mark for the first time. Confectionery consumption was £3,075 million, wine was second at £2,584 million, bread was £1,693 million and milk £1,621 million. In 1989, Terry's produced chocolates shaped like gold bars for sale at the Bank of England.

John Earnshaw recalls,

We had decided one thing that was strategically right was to have a sugar element to our business. When Terry's Group was formed within United Biscuits, later on in the '80s, they acquired Callard and Bowser. They had a Bridgend operation. I was part of the team that did a study exercise with consultants and recommended certain things because it was a very different culture and style. Then later we looked to bring the whole of the Bridgend operation into York 'cos part of our plan had been to flatten almost all production onto ground floor facilities and not use the multi-storey factory. That was ideal to put the Bridgend operation in. On this Friday my boss rang me and said, "It's all go". On Friday night, "It's all off". And somebody at the higher levels in the organisation had worried about the disruption to the business, because most of the Bridgend business was based in the States.

Richard Harte remembers,

United Biscuits put a tremendous amount of capital expenditure into the plant. They built a brand new chocolate mill. All the production of their chocolate biscuits went to Manchester, and we would tanker chocolate there from York.

When Terry's was built, it was a multi storey factory, the concept was that the production of the chocolate started on the top floor and gradually went down the different floors to packing and then it went out the gate. To change to a single storey business, there were tremendous costs in changing round. There's another argument that the best thing to be done was to sell the site and build a brand new factory to the right economy of scale. The old Terry family, if you look at the 1930s, the different varieties of chocolates that they had and the knowledge of chocolate and how it's made. I sometimes think we won't have any concept of what it tasted like.

Under United Biscuits, each factory had an Employee Relations Manager. And I became ours. So my role changed very much. Under Colgate Palmolive and Forte's we were a company, we had our own accounts department, marketing department, sales department, all based on that site. But we became just a production site, the marketing and sales offices had gone down to London.

Sir Hector Laing was a tremendously charismatic character, and he wanted to go to see the factory at Hemsworth, before it closed. He landed by helicopter and would take off and come to York, and be provided with lunch. I went out with my assistant to do this recce, where the helicopter was going to land. We took the wrong turning and had to turn round in this gateway, and were suddenly confronted by these miners! We stopped the car, and it's a frightening sight to see all these miners coming towards you, and they said, "Are you from the ambulance service?" Somebody had apparently collapsed and they'd sent for an ambulance. I had a company car at the time, and it was decided that my car would be at Hemsworth ready to pick up Sir Hector and take him to the factory. I had a golden Labrador and my car was covered in hairs, and I spent all weekend cleaning this out so it was absolutely perfect. It was taken to the site and I wasn't there because I was at York. And they'd stood there with all the doors open, waiting for the helicopter to land. They'd cut the grass, and what happens when the helicopter lands, you get the down draught, and all the grass went into the car. So everything I'd done was a complete and utter waste of time.

Mike Grimes explains,

Terry's were never going to be the same size as Cadbury's or Rowntree's, but they had some nice niche products, which disappeared off. At one time we had about 178 different products, from small bars to silver caskets of expensive chocolates. And we were having to store it for nine months, and we'd got money just laid idle. And that is when these small speciality brands were made at the quiet times of the year. Terry's philosophy was to always be at the niche end of the market, because the vision of the Terry family back in the '20s was to produce the quality product. Cadbury and Rowntree concentrated more on the mass market. New lines, in the United Biscuits period, never took off. The marketers never stayed with a product from start to finish. They would come up with an idea, we would produce it, but by the time we got it into the retailer, the people had moved on to another job.

All Gold had 22 different centres. There were creams, caramels, nougats, but now they're a variation on three things. Lemon was a real hot favourite at one time, you don't find many lemon flavoured centres now, cherry's disappeared, coffee's gone, ginger's gone. Mint you don't want to produce because you get the cross contamination of flavours. Production is not usually a big headache. The headaches came when they wanted to blend a number of centres together, like white, dark, milk, all at the same time, caramel in hard form, soft caramel, fudges and fondants. But technology is there these days, you can just about produce anything.

In the early days we used seventeen to twenty types of beans, from different parts of the world, blended together to give a particular flavour. But they started rationalising that and when I left they were making chocolate from one source of beans.

Each company had its own distinctive taste, because of the beans and the palette of their loyal clientele. It's the blending and roasting that produce the distinctive flavours. Now in the supermarkets, there's all these specialist tablets of chocolate and they're bringing back the high cocoa content, like on the Continent. The industry is coming full cycle, more and more chocolatiers are starting up in the UK.

Mike Grimes as Chocolate Orange with Rachel
Semlyen at a fundraising event 2000

(Courtesy Mike Grimes)

We had charity events, and one of the biggest things that they raised money for was the St Leonard's Hospice, something in the order of £8,000 a year towards them. United Biscuits matched us pound for pound. We organised Miss Terry competitions, and outings to T.V. studios. But when they sold the Clementhorpe factory, the bowling greens went, the tennis courts, the fishing rights on that side of the river. We had to start hiring facilities out for tennis and bowling and it became uneconomic.

1974 was the building of the main warehouse on the site, which was close on 9,000 square metres. Then the next major build was 1984 when they extended the single storey factory to accommodate new moulding plants. In 1986 they built the Bay 5 section, the new cocoa liquor processing plant. It was felt that production shouldn't take place under north light roofing and a project was generated to re-roof the factory, over the top of the existing building, and that was done in 1990. And we did one half of the single storey factory but unfortunately there was a changeover in ownership and they decided that capital wasn't available to do that anymore.

With United Biscuits centralising everything, all the major ingredients came from a central buying facility in Osterley. United Biscuits hoped to create a new export base after Terry's, under Colgate Palmolive, had lost the many established agencies built up over the years.

John Earnshaw recalls,

United Biscuits decided to bring in management consultants, McKinsey, to look at the business in a much wider scope. I was told I would spend 15 per cent of my time with them and 85 per cent doing my own job. And the result was I was spending 85 per cent of the time with them and 15 per cent doing the job, eight in the morning till ten at night, for nearly a year. But they added a lot of input and professionalism. They were real workaholics, they definitely earned their money. They made me Production Manager and I implemented the plans with the team. We had 120 non-working supervisors and in the plan that we'd put together, there was going to be six. So having to tell 100 or so people that their role was still there, but instead of walking up and down the line, they had to be part of the line, was an interesting challenge.

They understood that change was necessary, and most of the people did embrace it. Without their commitment it wouldn't have happened. It was a status thing and we were trying to take the status out. Until you were a certain level you could not use the front door. One of the first things I did was to remove the A and B canteen, change the situation for the front door, so that we had a receptionist and people who worked in the office didn't have to walk round. The directors and senior managers had parking under cover but we demolished the sheds and made it open parking. The whole thing was about team effort, and we create more if we're seen to be more equal.

Where Terry's really missed the boat, it was in looking ahead and seeing what was needed to develop the business. Terry's used to have a Curiously Strong Mint. We made half a ton a week. Now at Bridgend we were making 200 tons a week. We moved quite a lot of the office based people into the factory, so the office people supporting production were part of their team. In the past it was always, "This is what you're having to do", but now, "It's up to you to develop it in the way you want. And use the money wisely". There were times when I wasn't very popular. I had many battles with the shop stewards. But in my early years I spent time working on the shop floor with the people. And I think there was an element of trust.

There were some big characters in the early days. The Personnel Officer was Ron Collier. There used to be some personality battles but over time there was a mutual respect. I remember we were talking about when people were getting into trouble over minor things. And we found this book of disciplinaries. And there was

Ron Collier's name. [The Suspension Book revealed that in 1928 he was in the chemical lab and he got one and a half days suspension for 'climbing about the new building'].

Packing Boxed Assortments 1960s
(Courtesy Mike Grimes)

I think the real issue would have been investing in brands at a much earlier stage. When we were part of Terry's, our MD prided himself in the fact that we had one Sales and Marketing Manager. So there was no real development of brands for the market and no strategy to support it. It all went on Terry's very good name for quality. The thing that's changed and why the boxed assortments are diminishing, is the takeover by things like Heroes and Quality Street. Terry's made a lovely dessert assortment, absolutely beautiful but the economics of it just didn't work. When Terry's was more of a family business, there was a lot more social activities, like in the sporting arena, which brought people together more. As the business became integrated into the big multi-nationals, it became less and less. They didn't invest as much in people on a social side. The bowling green at Clementhorpe was used on a few occasions to host England matches. It was Cumberland turf which apparently was the bees' knees in their own pavilion. When the site was sold, the developers invited a couple of us to go down there and put some memorabilia in a tube into the wall. When somebody in 100 years time demolishes the wall, they'll find part of Terry's history.

CHAPTER TEN

THE FINAL YEARS

In 1990, there were 1500 full time employees at Terry's and 900 part-timers. The firm handled 10,000 tonnes of cocoa beans and won first and second prize for their Easter eggs that year in 'Food' magazine. All Gold had been worth £11 million in 1981 but had doubled by 1990.

At its peak, the company sold 23,000 tons of chocolate, 56 million Chocolate Oranges, (over one billion slices), and 650 tons of Easter eggs every year. They bought in white chocolate and Toblerone from the sister factory on the continent. By the early '90s, 65 per cent in the factory were now men, with students and mums making up the evening shift.

By this time, chocolate accounted for ten per cent of all the consumer food market. Terry's had always said, "We're in the happiness business". It was estimated that 15-24 year olds accounted for 24% of all purchases, so Terry's were working on new ways to appeal to this market. All Gold packaging and other products were significantly enhanced. There was ingot shaped packaging, a hexagonal box with a Victorian feel and portraits of York on the side, and the Moonlight box was produced in the shape of a dinner jacket, and had striking art nouveau illustrations.

A new £7 million moulding plant was built in 1991 predominantly for the new Moments line, with its seven offshoot products, though in the end it was not fully utilised. A major advertising campaign promoted Moments and Pyramint. In 1992, Terry's profits were 14.3% up on the last year, but then in 1993, 70 workers on short term contracts were laid off.

Anne Horner worked part-time from 1989 until 2002,

mainly in the packing department. It was rather scary because I'd never done factory work before and I didn't know what it was going to be like. They gave us training but you were expected to pick it up quite quickly. The half pound belt was the one I worked on. It was quite noisy with machines at either end that made up the boxes. The belt went along with empty trays and you put the chocolates in as they went by. Further on, machines closed the lids and put the cellophane on.

The belts ran at different speeds. And sometimes they would turn ours up and they'd realise it was too fast because people were missing the chocolates out. There was a lady at the end whose job was to fill in any that were missing. Sometimes they had to slow it down but they didn't like doing that. Sometimes an order had to be finished by a certain time so it was a bit tense. And you'd get the machines breaking down and that would hold things up.

When I first started, they ran a bonus system. And I suppose that's why sometimes they turned the belts up because the fulltime belt ran a bit faster and they got a higher bonus. But it was very good pay.

The work was repetitive. After two hours we got quarter of an hour's break, but you could end up with repetitive strain injury on your wrists and fingers.

You wore a white overall and a little peaked cap. Later on they decided to be more strict and we had to wear a blue hairnet underneath and every part of your hair had to be covered. Some of the men had shoes with steel toe caps if they were doing heavier work. I always wore a shoe that covered your foot properly, 'cos it was safer.

Then they decided they just wanted fulltime staff on the belts so they moved some to other areas. I was working where chocolates were actually made, coming off a moving belt and you had to catch them on trays. I saw the different procedures which was quite interesting. They often did a special box for All Gold, with a Christmassy design. I remember even the Easter eggs were changing, 'cos they used to do a lot of little novelty eggs for children. They could have made a lot more of the Easter egg sales if they'd been a bit more versatile. They did little bags of sweets and each one was like half a Chocolate Orange, and you made up a box like a cracker. You twisted one end and then the other and that was the one that made my thumb ache.

There was one lad in charge of mixing the centres and big plastic moulds. The bottom part of the chocolate shell would go in, then the filling and the top. That took up the whole length of one room. The chocolate just got everywhere and it would set, so you had to spend time cleaning the machine so that it would keep working. You always felt as if you smelt of chocolate all the time, it was in the atmosphere.

In the part where the chocolates were being made, they made a big crashing sound. And you were more likely to have got headaches in there. But then when you were sitting next to somebody on a packing belt, you could usually have a good conversation. Where the Waifa bars were, you were supposed to wear ear protectors. The machinery there was getting past its use by date. We'd have a lot of problems with it and they decided that would be made abroad. And they changed the recipe.

You sometimes felt that they hadn't kept the standards up as well as they once were. Some of the older women would talk about dusting chocolates to make sure they were shiny, the little finishing touches that had gone by the wayside. They were more concerned about output than these little details. They started to use more machinery that had computers attached and they introduced inkjet machines that shot the sell-by date onto boxes. They were always looking for ways of reducing staff.

I could sense this idea of the family firm to some extent, though there were gradual signs that you were just a number. If you had a full attendance for one year, they'd send you a letter, "Thank you very much for 100% attendance record, and we hope that you'll continue in our service for many years to come". I'd had this letter and two weeks later they announced that it was redundancies for all the part time staff. You could either take redundancy or go fulltime. So it was a bit upsetting. I wouldn't have wanted to do fulltime, to take on more hours.

But the thing that really sticks with me about Terry's was the social side, the friends. And I get quite emotional thinking about it. Working in a team you made such good friendships. And because it was boring work you could sit and chat about anything you wanted. I love different types of people and different characters, and that was what made it for me. And I've managed to keep in touch with people. But obviously it's never the same again when you've left. Even if the work wasn't all that interesting, the friendships that people made were very important to them and that was something that you could never replace.

Vic Botterill was born in 1946 and went to Terry's in 1973. Vic's brother, Mark, and son Paul worked there, and his daughter met her husband Darren Gray there.

When I first started, I was in the crystallised mints department then I was a fork lift driver. Then I was talked into being the shop steward because I was the one with the

gob. *After five years they decided that they wanted me to become Convenor or Chief Shop Steward and I was stuck with that up to the closure. Most of the time I spent talking with management and dealing with problems. Over the years as new technology took over and staff diminished, membership went down. I was representing the GMB, originally APEX, the office union, and GMB for blue collar workers. Then it all became one. Originally at Terry's you had the Tinsmith's Union, Electrician's Union, Mechanic's Union, there was about five different lots. Then they all came under the EETPU, with the engineers.*

The 1970s was a volatile time for industry.

It was not friendly. You had to fight, get your people behind you, to force issues. We've only had one strike with the shop floor at Terry's, because we were far behind the wages of Nestlé. And we'd sat in a meeting with our management for three days and at the end of it we came out with half a per cent. We got everybody behind us, and we ended up getting a 23 per cent rise. They wanted to save money, we wanted to improve our working conditions. And whereas it started off as a catfight between unions and management, eventually it was a partnership. We'd sit down, work out the best way to do it, and take it to the shop floor. For example, at one time you had factory fortnight where the factory shut down, so you had to book your holidays then, the most expensive time of year to go. We said we'd like to have our holidays at different times but we could run the factory all year round. It was hard work but we got it.

Before we went for a pay rise, our routine was that I would speak to every union member, each department. But no matter what you take them back, it's never enough. I'd say, "I've done the negotiations. Everything I've come back with is by talking. If you're not happy with that, you're the union, I'm just the mouthpiece. If the majority vote 'no', then I'm going to come back with a vote for industrial action". In the last ten years or so, people weren't prepared to take industrial action. They were frightened 'cos they didn't want to lose money. And because we did come back with reasonable offers, then they decided to accept it.

95 per cent were in the union. If they're in a union, there's the backup. And we had a couple of cases where managers had been over the coals and we sorted it out. At least 75 per cent of the managers were union members. Even some of the senior bosses.

I've always said that the highest paid people were the fork lift drivers. And all you did was sit and drive the fork lift round and at odd times you did have to haul stuff off wagons which was quite physical. But you get one of these drivers and you say, "I want you to sit and put chocolates in boxes eight hours a day", they couldn't do it. And those were the lowest paid. So we did a job evaluation scheme, took every job and put it into categories, physical wasn't the biggest point scorer, it was knowledge and this type of thing. But we got so the packers went higher up on the scale, the fork lift drivers came down a little bit. It equalised it a lot more. And then I'd say, "Let's have some women fork lift drivers", and eventually we got women to train. By the end we had 20 women drivers so that shows these barriers are broken down. On the moulding plants, it was male dominated, but by the end, it was 50/50. Wages improved in these areas and I think there was a lot of women becoming breadwinners. And a lot of the physical side had gone out of it. We introduced 12 hour working patterns, to keep up production and you could earn really good money.

Originally you had a manager, then you had team leaders. Over the years that developed and you cut the layers of management out. I was a party to changing a lot of that. Over the years, it was our main aim to improve things. We got our accident levels to nearly zero. No factory is ever safe to work in, but I would say it was one of the safest. We got an award for our safety.

But you've got to have respect for your workforce. You can rule with an iron fist and you'll have no respect whatsoever and the first chance your people get, they'll drop you right in it. But you treat them with respect and talk to them, they'll do anything for you.

I used to run the football team, we actually won the league at one stage. If we wanted a kit, the money was there for us. As the years went on, our footballers got older and the young ones weren't coming through. It got to the point where I had to kick it into touch. So all the football kit, we give it to youth clubs.

We had darts, dominoes, inter departmental knockouts. They played snooker daily in the canteen. If I went to them for money for certain things, like the football pitch, we used to get it. People would pay five pence a week into a fund, for snooker tables in the canteen, table tennis tables, fishing rods.

Josie Black in canteen
(Courtesy Geoff Spence)

Under United Biscuits they got rid of our drivers. Our security people were made redundant and then our cleaning staff, contractors were brought in. The only thing we held onto was the canteen. Going back five or ten years there was a divide between the tradesmen and the shop floor. But then multi-skilling came in. That meant that a lot of the mediocre jobs went onto the shop floor. So demarcation had to be stopped. If there was a machine went wrong and it jammed, that could be done by the plant operators. The shop floor got better paid because they got more multi-skilled. With Chocolate Orange, when I first started, there was 250 people in that department, at the end there was six people producing 20 times as much. When I took over as convenor, we had 16 shop stewards. It got down to six at the end.

[In 1937 men earned 56 shillings for a 47 hour week] *and in 2000 it was £230 for a 39 hour week on the packing belt.*

Tony Coward left at this time.

In 1992, United Biscuits had a big shake-up and our MD went to look after the biscuit company. And another chap was appointed, Brian Cardie, and he and I just did not get on. He was a marketing man whereas I had been a manufacturing man and felt the biggest asset was the people. Then they offered me various out posts with the company, 'keep your salary and car…or you can have a package'. That sounded very attractive and I left. Three months later, Terry's Group was sold to Kraft and all the directors went. I like to think I had something to do with the appointment of John Earnshaw and definitely with John Pollock and they ended up running the factory.

I absolutely loved my career until the last two years and that was purely a clash of personalities. They were financially the best years, but I was living in an aeroplane, hard work but fun.

In 1990, Kraft Foods, a division of Philip Morris, had bought Jacobs Suchard, (founded 1826) and in April 1993 came the third takeover for Terry's, as they merged to create the UK's fourth largest manufacturer, Kraft Jacobs Suchard, based in Cheltenham. The cost was £220 million. It was Europe's second largest confectionery company. The chocolate manufacture remained at York, sugar confectionery was at Bridgend in Wales. They also had continental style chocolate in Austria, France, Germany, Switzerland and Scandinavia. Toblerone and Suchard provided a continental flavour, with the Dime bar for the teenage market.

Under Kraft, benefits to employees included a central sports organisation, chiropodist, free legal advice, (solicitors visited once a month), and financial rewards for good suggestions.

John Earnshaw recalls the changes.

When we were Terry's and had our own sales force and they were visiting all the smaller shops, it made sense to have the portfolio products. As we moved into Kraft, they had central negotiations for sales. They only dealt with the big people and were only interested in big brands. When you're competing against Cadbury's Dairy Milk, people in the UK are weaned on it. They've got the whole thing right. The chocolate drop when you're very young to the chocolate bars later on. The cost of entry into that market is huge, and the chances of success very limited. Terry's never really had a chance.

We could make a chocolate bar, similar to Cadbury's Dairy Milk but it would be Tesco's. You could make a Mars Bar for Marks and Spencer's and that's the sort of thing we'd do. Under United Biscuits you'd got young marketing people telling us what to do. It was a completely different concept to what they'd been used to. They began to make a Chocolate Orange bar, because you get one main brand and the derivatives from that, and that's what used to happen. They produced various seven day wonders really. Pyramint was one, a plain chocolate with a peppermint centre. 'Moments' was another, and 'Erasures', bars with soft centres in the middle.

When we were taken over, the chief shop steward said that he didn't want to go on much longer. And I said, "I think if we're going to take this forward, you're going to have to commit to spending three or four years 'cos there's going to be a lot of change, we need experienced people that they look up to". Vic did very well. His job was harder than many of the managers and he'd got to have courage. But when a corner needed to be fought, he was willing to fight it. I think he did play a good part.

The first management cluster was Kraft in Europe. We just had one factory director, one finance, one HR [Human Resources] and local management teams. Sometimes we were in Bridgend, sometimes we were on the road. We were in an operational structure that was European based. And my boss was in Belgium. If Terry's was to stay in York, the only thing we could do was to use that site to its full. And yet the only way we could compete in operations, we had to reduce our dependency on the multi-storey, and get it down to single storey operation.

I was Confectionery Operations Director for Kraft in the UK. At Bridgend, we worked hard, turned that factory round, extended the production lines, increased sales to the States. I'd go over to New Jersey and work with the team there. We geared up production to such a level that the next generation was going to be something special. And Kraft decided to change the way that we managed the business in the States. They integrated a small team that were basically Callard and Bowser operating within Kraft and the business collapsed. There wasn't the specialist knowledge, the people who were working with the brokers. Bridgend started to fall, and we had to reduce what was a 24 hour operation into a 12 hour one. We developed further products to support the business but there wasn't the real focus so we consolidated down to a smaller size and got it back up to the level that it was before. They announced they were selling virtually all of the sugar businesses to Wrigley's. But the day after they took over, they went down and closed it. I felt really sorry for the Bridgend people because they'd been through so much. And they were absolutely brilliant.

Kraft had some of the best training, to help people become self sufficient, team building operations where we took people off the line and supported them in developing the way they could work. It was training that not only you could use in business, but you could use in life. The best training was when we were doing the management buyout. Whatever happens in my life, I'll think of all the things that we did to try and make a business. We'd say, we need to get MAD, 'Make a Difference'.

John had to deal with redundancies.

There's a lot of soul searching goes on. I think at the end of the day you recognise for the greater good of the total business, it has to happen. You try and distance yourself from the emotions of it but emotions come through, 'cos you know the people. It's tough but we recognised that if you're going to survive, you've got to make harsh decisions and just make sure that you are as human as you possibly can be. At the end of the day, it's all about people. And people really do matter. And I think there've been some fantastic people in the confectionery industry, some really great ones at York.

The Senior Management Team 1993
L to R – Maria Dineen (Technical Manager), John Pollock (Financial Controller),
John Earnshaw (Factory Director), John Preston (Engineering Manager),
Kath Stacey (Factory Efficiency Manager),
Jonathan Metcalf (HR and Training Development Manager) and
Ian Forman (Product Engineering Manager)
(Courtesy Mike Grimes)

When in 1995, 100 redundancies were announced, over 200 people applied. 200 jobs were axed in 1996. In 1998 a new production line was built. But it did not save the company.

In 2000, Waifa production went to Belgium. Two years later, 40 jobs were axed following the fall in exports to the USA. By this time the writing was on the wall. In January 2004, Kraft announced cuts of 6000 jobs worldwide and in April, finally announced that Terry's was to close with the loss of 316 jobs. By this time only half the buildings were actually occupied.

The Press in York launched a campaign to 'Save Terry's'. The petition, with more than 4,700 signatories, was presented by chief reporter Mike Laycock, Labour MP Hugh Bayley, GMB organiser John Kirk and three factory workers – Wayne Foster, Darren Gray and Carole Cooper. Peter Terry and eight other members of the family had signed it. But unfortunately it did not change anything.

The last pensioners' Christmas dinner took place in 2004 at York Racecourse when 400 met together.

Peter Terry said to the gathering,

> It was the saddest day of my life when I heard Terry's was going to close. In a year's time Terry's of York will be no more. To think that Terry's products are being made abroad and shipped back here under our name, it should never have happened. It breaks my heart to see it. It's sad for the history of York, the traditions and the people of York and of course the employees. It can never be changed. It's gone from York forever.

And everybody stood up and cheered him.

The Press and Radio York were inundated with emails from all over the world. A man from Cape Town wrote,

> I was 'absolutely devastated to find we are unable to buy the wonderful Terry's Chocolate Orange any more, and more devastated that the factory is closing down. What a huge loss'.

Keith, an ex-pat from Canada, wrote,

> 'Terry's chocolate was always preferred by my family. What a lovely confection. When I came here and courted young Canadian ladies, I introduced them to Terry's especially at Christmas'.

Gordon from Florida wrote,

> 'Terry's chocolate is an institution. I am devastated that this wonderful product is no longer available. More tragic is the loss to hard working employees'.

A man named Ian said,

'My grandfather and grandmother met and fell in love at Terry's. It has been a family tradition to give Terry's chocolates at Christmas but now Terry's effectively does not exist'.

By this time production of All Gold had already gone to Sweden. The plant was making Chocolate Orange for the last few months before switching to Poland and Slovakia. York Fruits had moved to Zagreb in Croatia and Twilights were being made in Austria. The packaging now reads 'Made in the EU'. But one of the last employees said,

"As well as leaving your job, you are leaving your friends, it's been like a second family".

Terry's finally closed on 30th September 2005. The television advert for Chocolate Orange had featured comedian Dawn French saying, 'It's not Terry's, it's mine'. Now the headline read, 'It's not Terry's, it's not anybody's'. A sad reflection on the end of an era.

Terry's Spring 2006. The last Chocolate Orange is presented to Peter Terry. L to R – Tony Coward, John Earnshaw, Peter Terry, John Pollock, Ian Johnston, all at one time directors.

(Courtesy Anne Ruttle)

Only a few months after Terry's closed, Peter Terry died in February 2006. The York Civic Trust Report read, 'Peter enriched the lives of all who knew him, and made significant and lasting contributions to the city he loved'.

In 2005, five factory buildings at Terry's became Grade II Listed, the head office in its Baroque Revival style, the liquor factory, clock tower, water tower and boiler house. Kraft gave all the photographs from the '50 Years Gallery' to relatives, and the premises were gradually cleared. Grantside Developments bought the site for £26 million in 2006.

Mike Grimes remembers,

> Gordon MacIlroy, a chap who I worked with for 33 years, ended up as chief engineer. I was his project engineer. And there were only the two of us left in the end, he was the last employee still left in the factory, and he signed on the dotted line, and handed the keys to the new owner.

Grantside's business plan to bring the former works to life was rejected by York City Council in July 2008, despite recommendation by council officers. A new plan was submitted in August 2009, after months of discussions with local residents and the council. They also worked with York Racecourse to ensure the sites complement each other.

The aim is to create 2,700 jobs, with new homes, hotels, shops, restaurants, nursery and medical centre. The Managing Director Steve Davis said he was delighted that they have been able to produce a completely fresh application and that the variety would create a 'vibrant and sustainable development'. York's Chamber of Commerce commented, "We cannot stress our support enough. This is an iconic site and part of the city's identity. It is hugely important to the future economy of the city". Terry's was once the heart of a community. Grantside are trying to make it so again. As this book goes to print, they await the council's decision.

'Terry's of York' is no more. The company had come a long way since those early days of Joseph Terry and Bayldon and Berry, producing their cough lozenges and sweetmeats for the gentry in Georgian York, and filling their ledgers using quill pens by the light of a candle. In the course of 240 years, thousands of men and women had been proud to be known as part of Terry's, whether making or packing chocolates, typing or invoicing in the vast and noisy office, working as fitters, electricians, plumbers and engineers; or designing and marketing new products, taking them on the road to department stores, corner shops, hotels and theatres; providing delicious meals in Terry's restaurant and front shop, catering for weddings and society functions, or running the business from the board room, each one had a part to play, each person had a significant role. Their stories are a part of the history of York, and though now gone, they are not forgotten.

BIBLIOGRAPHY

Confectioners' Union magazine. 14th June 1930

Confectionery in Perspective. The Cocoa, Chocolate and Confectionery Alliance. 1979

Food Magazine. Articles 'Terry's of York'. December 1950 and February and March 1952

Merchandising Vision. Volume 2. British Cellophane Ltd. 1979

The Life and Times of Edward Peart Brett. Colin Sheppard. York Historian 25. 2008. Yorkshire Architectural and York Archaeological Society

Terry's of York 1767-1967. Privately published for Terry's. 1967

United Biscuits Teams. Article by Ian Binks. United Biscuits News. May 1982

York Races programme for Terry's All Gold Ebor. 20th August 1975

Yorkshire Business June 1990, article on Terry's by Jim Gibbins. Yorkshire Post Newspapers

Yorkshire Evening Press, now The Press

Yorkshire Gazette